What Others are Saying

What have I learnt? Moji is richer and deeper than I have ever imagined. While I understand this to be a memoir, it is a huge comfort to me as a first-generation immigrant that in this book, Moji was able to clearly show how the challenges we face in integrating into a new environment and culture are nothing but stepping stones and a means to reaffirm our decisions to call Canada home. Moji never allowed her experiences to embitter her to any race or people. I have learned that one or two or many bad experiences do not mean that a people group are all the same or should be painted with the same brush.

I always knew Moji was special but reading this explains why, and now I do understand why she has cheered me on so loudly.

I truly loved reading this book. It is a well-written and engaging page-turner. Moji has opened a door into her life for everyone to see. It is amazing how she could find a way to incorporate her generosity into every aspect of her life, and she continues to do that to this very day. She has always been a giver, leaving a piece of herself in every life she meets. Her legacy lives on in the lives of family and friends alike.

I recommend this book to everyone. To immigrants, it portrays the mindset that triumphs over the negativity that one is bound to experience in settling into a new culture, and to indigenous locals, it brings one face-to-face with the effect that bigotry has on your fellow humans.

Dr. Olubunmi Oyebanji, Family Physician; Calgary, Alberta, Canada

It is a privilege and an honour to be asked to write a brief review of this autobiography of Mrs. Moji Taiwo, a leading Nigerian-Canadian citizen, who is firmly dedicated to serving and impacting society positively. She is a rare combination of altruism, beauty, brain and brawn.

I Give Because I'm Blessed, I'm Blessed Because I Give is not only a breath of fresh air for any reader, but a validation of the truth found in the late Lucky Dube's song[1] that good things come to those who go out and make them happen. As I read through the manuscript, I was faced with the difficulty of how best to succinctly describe for the reader the experience of a 20-year-old, single, Nigerian lady who dared to migrate to Canada in the late 1970s, confronting headlong the challenges of life in a culturally different and sometimes perceived discriminatory environment, yet making a tremendous success of the process.

The author's experience on arrival in Canada would resonate with a large number of educated individuals who left the African continent for sojourn in other parts of the world,

---

[1] Lucky Dube. "Good Things", *Taxman* [1997]

especially Europe and North America. The memoir reiterates the rude awakening most African immigrants have faced on arrival at their destinations. First, the cultural as well as environmental shock of the vast disparity between what they were accustomed to and the adjustment to be made for integration into the host community. Second, the absence of communal sustainment they were used to in Africa, which in Nigerian parlance translates to the phrase "you are on your own". While you may find pockets of charity and generosity for the first few days on arrival, this may not be a long-time gesture as everyone is struggling to survive and succeed. As such, your failure or success is down to your individual efforts and ability to surmount all challenges. You become the sole author of your own destiny. Third, the expectation that their qualifications which they believed were equivalent to any in Africa and the western world would get them into the corridors of professional employment are dashed. The reality on arrival when employments are found – being as cleaners or security guards – becomes a huge shock. As the author succinctly put it, "I had successfully held an office job. Here, I was trading my expertise and experience for a cleaning job."

Beyond the story of focus, courage, determination, perseverance, and success as an immigrant in Canada that are replete in the memoir, the author imparts a number of life skills that could serve as a foundation for success. For example, referencing her thirty-eight-years of marriage to Aderinola Taiwo, it can be deduced that a happy marriage does not depend on either how rich the parties are or how long the courtship between a man and a woman is, but on how sincere, committed, and supportive they are of each other's aspirations. Furthermore, throughout the memoir, it becomes evident that the author's progress in gradually building a successful career in Canada as well as a happy home hinged on the consistency to re-assess, re-evaluate, and re-adjust her modalities to ensure the goals she and her husband had set themselves became reality. In essence, once they set their goals, they constantly re-adjusted the sails of their ship as the weather dictated to ensure that they arrived successfully at the port of their destination.

I recommend this autobiography to:

1. Prospective immigrants – as it enables them to birth their expectations in a new country in reality;

2. Existing immigrants – as the story of Moji's struggles and achievements may resonate with some people, whilst encouraging those immigrants still seeking to reach their goals that they will make it if they do not give up;

3. The general public, particularly non-immigrant Canadians – for an understanding of what it means to be an immigrant: the discouragements and strength of character that goes with breaking through human barriers in a challenging environment;

4. Canadian policy makers – towards identifying means and processes that enhance the arrival and existential experiences of immigrants in Canada.

This memoir is about focus, courage, and success in a new land. In it, I have found a practical guide for my mentees on building a career using project management tools and processes.

Conclusively, I will describe the author, Moji Taiwo with these words: daring, fearless, focused, courageous, dedicated, persevering, successful, and contented.

Olukunle Ojeleye, PhD; Calgary, Alberta, Canada

I'm Blessed is the story of Moji, the story of an independent woman who emigrated from Lagos, Nigeria, to Calgary, Canada, in the seventies, a time when Southern Alberta was still a very homogeneous society. The book tells of the cultural shock she faced in terms of climate, language, and social norms, of her encounters with both racism and welcome, and of her determination to always forge ahead. Moji meets Derin soon after she arrives in Calgary, and together, they endure the difficulties of concurrently working, raising a family, and going to school. The narration is funny and poignant at the same time, and embeds you, the reader, right along with her as she goes through life's experiences in her adopted country of Canada.

This book is a really good read for anyone who wants to know what it's like to be a new immigrant that grows into a contributing citizen – a citizen with a strongly developed sense of service.

Carlton Osakwe, PHD; Mount Royal University; Calgary, Alberta, Canada

One of the first things that jumped out at me about Moji's book was that it felt like she was pulling out a story from within me. It was not just her story, but it was an inspiring account of what many of us have to walk into, work with, and work through to get to where we want to be.

Moji's authentic writing style would connect with just about anyone, and this book could become the how-to manual for anyone planning on embarking on a similar journey.

"A mentor is someone who allows you to see the hope inside yourself."[2] (Oprah Winfrey) Moji Taiwo is a mentor.

Wale Balogun, Wealth Management Consultant; Calgary, Alberta, Canada

I Give Because I'm Blessed, I'm Blessed Because I Give was very interesting. It shows the need to make tough decisions in order to forge ahead in life.

In her story, Moji needed to get out of her first job despite not having any hope of getting a new job. That was a good

---

[2] Source: An interview with Oprah Winfrey on WCVB-TV 5 News *CityLine* (Boston, January 13, 2001).

decision because she had to let go of what she had in order to get new opportunities.

Moji's determination to follow her dream was without bounds. I love that she set goals and worked towards accomplishing her goals.

Jane Eruchalu, M.Sc. P.Eng; Calgary, Alberta, Canada

For those who have met Moji like I have, they will find it difficult to separate her personal traits in real life from how she has written her first book. Blunt. Frank. Without pretense. This is the most potent book by an immigrant that I have read. She clearly puts her story in the most candid manner.

In this book you will find, in practical terms, how courage, boldness, and resiliency can help you achieve your goals. Moji uses this book to teach us how to turn every mistreatment to a positive, every setback to triumph, how to reap from valuable connections, and that even in retirement, there shouldn't be a dull moment. With Moji, every skill learned was never wasted; it was always needed along the way.

I am practically thrilled about the sharpness of her memory in remembering names of those she worked with several years ago, including what transpired between them.

In Chapter 8, Moji gave me a big takeaway. In her words, "Part of being successful is recognizing that a closed door is sometimes the best thing that could happen to you."

A book like this is rare. It will inspire every immigrant, no matter where they come from.

Olajide Olutuyi, Calgary, Alberta, Canada

This is an attractive, compelling, and honest story with a clear layout, beautiful photographs, and cultural details.

Moji was destined to be special from a young age. With a humble and cosmopolitan upbringing, she showed early signs of her remarkable strong character. This is a beautiful book about accepting yourself and others for who they are and of embracing the unknown and life's challenges head on by turning what seems to be another barrier into a lesson and an opportunity.

This book is recommended for anyone going through changes in their life – those who need to adjust to new circumstances and let go of all that does not serve them – as it provides stories of finding your strength and the time to give service.

Faiza Farah; Calgary, Alberta, Canada

I Give Because I'm Blessed, I'm Blessed Because I Give offers readers an insight into the life of Mrs. Taiwo and her very interesting life in Canada. It is an honest, funny, and eye-opening, good read that captivates the readers and keeps you reading until the end. Mrs. Taiwo is very open in sharing her many life lessons, new discoveries, the many struggles to be accepted and fit in to a new country, as well as her various friendships and lifelong relationships. She is also candid and open to sharing her heart: hurts, joys, and love.

A very well done job, Mrs. Taiwo, for such an inspiring book.
Dee Adekugbe; All Woman Ministry; Calgary, Alberta, Canada

This is an amazing book, written with a free-flowing style and the art of a skilled storyteller. It takes off with how a single, young, Nigerian lady ventured to Canada with high hopes in search of the "golden fleece" and a brighter future. She went through the usual, initial challenges of an immigrant, especially of African descent. Virtually every immigrant can relate to the challenges, which include: language barriers or communication difficulties, lack of direction as to how to navigate the social, economic, and political landscapes, systemic blockade of access to quality, professional jobs, workplace politics, prejudice, culture shock, and racial discrimination.

Thankfully enough, every cloud has a silver lining. Moji discovered kind-hearted Canadians and others who were like guardian angels, helping her in her journey. This probably explains why sister Moji and family are deeply involved in community matters as a way of helping newcomers to find their feet by linking them to relevant professionals or even providing material support for the newcomer.

Her disappointments form part of her pillar of success. While she was not able to make a career in broadcasting due to prejudice and no thanks to her accent, her journalism training gave her a real boost in her ultimate profession in the young offenders' criminal justice system.

She devoted a whole chapter on what goes on within the criminal justice system and how the youth at risk are assisted through the process of stabilization, mentorship, and discipline for ultimate family and community reintegration.

Her strategic planning skills are commendable. She found love the very first year of arrival in "cold country Canada" and raised a beautiful family with her husband Derin amidst continuous efforts at shooting for the heights.

We recommend this book for three groups of readers:

1. Newcomers are encouraged not to be deterred by the initial obstacles, to make their goals, and to continue to follow through.

2. For parents of teenage and young children, it will give them an idea of what takes children into the system. It will help them to know how to keep them off criminality, and if already there, it may provide the way to assist them in showing support.

3. Group home clients should have the opportunity to read this. It might change the lives of some.

Philip & Olubunmi Latilo; Calgary, Alberta, Canada

WOW is what comes to mind after reading this book! With thoughtful insights and personal experience, Moji Taiwo has sung the song most people have not been able to do. You can always be blessed by the power of giving. Writing this book is truly a blessing to all immigrants and their families.

Ms. Taiwo has taken a bold step writing this book. She gives an insight into the struggles and successes of a black woman living in a foreign country. Ms. Taiwo is indeed a woman with an embodiment of testimonies of which I can attest to as a black woman myself growing up in Calgary.

Tokunbo Davidson; Realtor – Century 21 Bravo Realty; Calgary, Alberta, Canada

I have finished reading the first four chapters of Moji's book, and I cannot wait to read the entire novel! Her story is empowering on so many levels. She is an inspiration, not only to new immigrants to Canada, but to anyone who reads her life story. It goes to show how perseverance and determination will help guide you through life's encounters.

The manner in which she details her arrival in Canada and the challenges she faced kept me glued to the pages. She takes the reader through a journey, making them feel like they are right alongside her as she walks through her life's story.

Prior to reading this, I still knew Moji as this incredible, caring, and amazing woman, but to get a glimpse into her world gave me a better appreciation of who she is as a person.

Thank you, Moji, for sharing your story with everyone.

Clare Smart, Sgt.; Calgary, Alberta, Canada

From the very beginning, this book took me on a journey that evoked my personal adventure to Canada as a new immigrant. There was a poignant sense of deja vu – that feeling of living through similar experiences, including the sheer fright of knowing that you are leaving all that is familiar and comforting behind to embark on a journey to an unknown destination. There's an apprehension that you do not know who, what, or where you are going and there's the helplessness of being at the mercy of strangers who you hope will empathize and not lead you astray.

The first chapter, like the rest of the book, grips you and sucks you in, and you cannot help but keep turning the pages to see what comes around the corner. It is vintage Aunty Moji and captures her essence of courage, unconventionality, optimism, and joie de vivre – an exuberant enjoyment of life – along with the dancing, which she still does today at any party that she attends, and her ongoing love affair with Uncle Derin.

She displays an honesty and fidelity with the readers by telling her story the way it happened without any embellishments.

As I continued to read, I was in no doubt once again that this book is indeed written by my favorite Aunty! She did not let the overt racism, discrimination, and unjust treatment take her into the victimhood zone. She fought as best as she could, left the toxic environment and more importantly made a decision to position herself with her husband to help other immigrants by getting involved in the real estate business. The trailblazing nature and activism can be seen even just in the act of not watching the TV program of the anchorman that wrote her off so blithely without considering that perhaps education is an opportunity to learn and should not be denied to people deserving of the opportunity for a reason as trivial as an "accent"!

In the depth of all the challenges she faced, Aunty still remained resolute in focusing on her goals, dreams, opportunities, and especially on the people that she was privileged to develop binding and caring friendships with. It is also remarkable that these are lifetime friendships, as she is loyal and honors the privilege of friendship with these exceptional people.

I found Chapter 2 to be very special. Loly makes her entrance into the lives of this young couple struggling to get a head start in their brave, new life in their new country. It also chronicles the start of a new career path different from the original goals, and encapsulates the realization that this choice would still provide an outlet for Aunty's innate need to make a positive difference in the lives of the people that she meets especially the young. This is really the foundation of the work that binds Aunty to our hearts and the hearts of the young in our community. Her commitment to youth life skills acquisition and holistic wellbeing through the various youth programs that she anchors for the Nigerian Canadian Association in Calgary is legendary. The comfort levels that our youth enjoy with her are evident in the candid interactions with them and trust they have in her that she will guide them without being judgmental. She is indeed the cool but tough Aunty "who knows what time it is!"

Chapter 4 captivated me. It tells us about the struggles, challenges, victories, and provides the affirmation that there are indeed good people in the world. She gives credit to her friends, mentors, and champions who aided her in her journey. It reaffirms our belief that there is justice and the merits of tenacity in the face of adversity. Here we see the foundation of an amazing career and life dedicated to helping young people, including those in the correctional system by helping them see that there is more to them than whatever bad things that they have encountered or perpetrated in their past. It is a story of redemption.

A woman's struggle to balance the demands of working with the burgeoning needs of a young family are in stark view in this chapter. In her characteristic manner, Aunty Moji forges ahead to get on with it. She is in charge of her life and choices. She is meticulous at work and continuously invests in her personal development. She is not willing to settle and pragmatically takes on situations with a creed that she must overcome. She is present and she listens to her intuition, which guides her well during her career, especially as a very visible minority in the work place.

Conclusion: I see this book not as one book but as a prelude to many others. I will not say that the stories are incompletely told. Rather, they are shared in a way that leaves the reader with so many "aha" moments that bring on the urge to say, "Can there be more...please?"

This book is an ode to a journey of sheer will to thrive no matter the daunting odds. There is no apology for blazing a trail different from that trodden by people that came before. It is a testament to the "why not if not" philosophy. It is an ode to daring to dream and live differently. This Aunty Moji has done, always on her own, indomitable terms.

Mrs. Njide Harris-Eze; President – Nigerian Canadian Association Calgary; Calgary, Alberta, Canada

I GIVE

because

I'M BLESSED

• • • • • • • • • • • • • • • • • •

I'M BLESSED

because

I GIVE

Moji Taiwo

Published by Moji Taiwo
www.mojitaiwo.com

Cover Design and Layout by: ChristianAuthorsGetPaid.com

Editor: Cheryl Regier
Zachariah House – zachariahhouseofhelps@gmail.com

Cover Photo – Credit: Hero Images

Email: info@mojitaiwo.com *or* mojitaiwo1@gmail.com
Telephone: 1-403-618-8384
Facebook: Moji Taiwo (Public Page)

DISCLAIMER
This is the author's life story, and thus, the information, opinions, and accounts herein represent her personal records, memories, and perspective about the subjects disclosed and the people involved. She has made every effort to relay the details to the best of her recollection and knowledge. As such, as well as due to the sensitivity of some of the stories recounted in this personal account, some names have been changed in the book to protect identities.
Although the author speaks from her years of experience and extensive expertise, she does not assume any liability for any loss, risk, or injury (physical, emotional, mental, or financial) incurred by any individuals mentioned within (whose identities are duly protected) or by those who read the information enclosed.

Printed in the United States of America

ISBN – 978-1-7751235-0-7 (softcover)
ISBN – 978-1-775-1235-1-4 (e-book)

Dedication

To my parents,
Musendiq and *Munirat Balogun*

For giving me life

and

providing me with all the necessities

for living life well

Acknowledgements

Many people have supported me throughout my life and up to this moment of recounting my story, including family and friends, people whom I have met casually through various community involvements and my profession, and people who have felt that my story was and is worth telling

I would like to especially thank my family…

My faithful, loving, and supportive husband, Aderinola: He has, both consciously and unconsciously, come alongside me on my journey, staying by my side for 39 years so far. I appreciate your devotion and love you dearly!

My children: My daughters, Ololade and Adejoke (along with their spouses), and my son, Adedeji, have always openly listened to my next ideas, the next home projects, and  the next community projects. They have never doubted their strong-willed, high energy (and at times irritating), high-achieving mother. Thank you for your enduring patience and trust. I am forever proud to be called your mom.

My beautiful angels and grandchildren: Ezra (also known as Sr. Munchkin) and Caxton (also known as Jr. Munchkin). It was your births that put the necessary spark into my soul to put words down on to paper for you as you grow from little tykes to mature, strong, intelligent, loving, kind, compassionate human beings.   Since the start of this book project, Derin and I have been blessed with another grandbaby – Amos – brother to Ezra. Glamma loves you all very much!

My sisters and brothers: I appreciate you all for being surrogate parents to me when I was much younger and for encouraging and supporting my development. I am forever indebted to my older sisters for occasionally helping me escape my mother's whipping rod.

My parents: Without them, I would not exist. They gave me a solid foundation rooted in honesty, kindness, compassion, hard work, and self-assurance. May your spirits continue to watch over me from above.

A huge thanks to all the people – **my teachers, mentors, and friends** – who believed in and assisted me in whatever goal I needed to achieve…

I would like to recognize the following such individuals: Ian Mandin (RIP), Thelma (RIP), Lynda Harris, Gloria Haddow (RIP), Mitch Bechtold, Chester Uszacki, Eileen Kwan, Loni Melvin,

Barbara Mcknight, Ramona Deer, Bill Pratt (RIP), Frank Vorstermans, and Karen Ferguson.

Thanks to Bill Pratt, Dr. Tony Kakpovbia, Dennis Waronuk, Jennifer Forster, Ben and Makda for the open doors they provided for my children, providing them with valuable job experiences that assisted them in achieving future success. To Jeff Pentz, thank you for talking to your neighbor who connected my son to his boss at Shaw Communications. The rest is history, as the saying goes.

An immense thank you goes out to my community brother and sister friends who are too numerous to list them all by name in this book. Just know that you are greatly appreciated. Yet, there are a few I would like to mention specifically: Joshua Adeoshun, Wale and Bernie Gbalajobi, Osita Nwofor, Dr. Julius Ogunnariwo, Wale Onabadejo, Steve Anene, Cypril Ekwulugo (RIP), Dr. Samuel and Regina Oluwadairo, Dr. Ben Nzekwu and Vikki Nzekwu (RIP), Lawrence Daramola, Mona Okafor (RIP), Adenike Olagundoye, Agnes Ibelo, Easter Metuh, Grace Oyelusi, Roseline Adeniyi, Eunice Omotosho, Florence Adereti, Dr. Samuel Afolayan, Mr. Peter and Dr. Bunmi Oyebanji, Sina and Sola Akinsanya, Dr. Yinka and Mrs. Yinka Marcus, Elizabeth Arnellien, and Sandra Ryan-Robinson. I love you all!

Thanks to all our realtors, financial advisors, mortgage brokers, and especially, our accountant, Vincent Duberry, for helping my husband and I plan, execute, and achieve our personal and business, financial goals.

And a mighty thank you goes to those of you who believed in me enough to encourage me to put my uniqueness onto these pages, including Dee (Adeola) Adekugbe who introduced me to my fabulous, author's coach and hounded me to get going on this project, and Paul Amanoh who casually announced, "You should write a book," as we discussed life in Canada.

A special note of gratitude goes to Catherine Kakpovbia, a sister friend, who graciously took my book-writing project and helped me transfer it from a confused and jumbled collection of notebook entries into chapters ready for the editing process and who provided clarifications and suggestions in the process. Thank you from the deepest part of my heart.

To my editor, Cheryl Regier, whose methodic and creative ways of extracting the finest of details from me onto pages, thank you for your keen interest in my book and for always reminding me that I needed to reach audiences beyond my immediate circle(s) with this book. I appreciate you and your craft.

Thanks to Kathleen Mailer, my author's coach, for unlocking my memory bank onto several pages within an hour of meeting with you. Your positivity is infectious, your energy uplifting!

Finally, and most importantly, **I give the greatest glory to my Creator** for all the blessings bestowed upon me so far along with the abilities and opportunities to share those gifts with others!

Foreword

I have had the privilege of knowing Moji ("Aunty Moji" as she is fondly called in the Nigerian community in Calgary) through one of her community service initiatives, Women of Vision. For me, one word that sums up Moji is "model". Moji is a model in every sense of the word, not because of her commitment to professional modeling following her retirement from 31 years of public service, but because of her unique character and qualities that set her apart from others. Moji inspires, motivates, and brings out the best in humanity. She is a born leader with a heart of gold. Her natural attributes draw people to her like a magnet.

Resilient, fearless, mentor, role model, great teacher, progressive leader, honest, strong work ethic, positive and approachable, dependable, achiever, agile, systems thinker, creative problem-solver, dedicated and committed, strong and passionate, caring and compassionate, intelligent with a quick wit and sense of fun – these are some of the words and phrases used to describe Moji. For those of you who have met Moji in person, I need not go further. For those of you who have not, these testimonials provide just a sketch of the amazing woman you are about to meet in the following pages.

As a doctorate degree holder, I have read many books, including autobiographies, in my lifetime. But I have not, until now, encountered a book so empowering like Moji's life story. This book recounts an amazing life journey of an ambitious, 19-year-old, black girl who arrived in Canada with big dreams and aspirations from Nigeria in West Africa, only to discover that Canada had no room for black women in the professional domain in the 1970s.

Moji's unique qualities, with which she withstood both the thick and thin over several decades, are vividly poured out in nine chapters of captivating personal stories that flow into each other with intriguing thrill and suspense. The intensity of the challenges along her way, the tenacity with which she tackled and overcame them, her determination to positively impact people's lives, her commitment to family, and her passion for service make her story exceptionally inspirational. Her dashed dreams of a career in broadcast journalism did not deter Moji in any way. As you will read in the following pages, she quickly re-plotted her career path in the humanities field, and in 1984, commenced a profession in public service as a youth worker in Alberta's Ministry of Justice and Solicitor General Correctional Services Division, Young Offender Branch. Moji arduously rose up the ranks, surmounting all obstacles to become one of the very few women to attain a management position as a Deputy Director of Operations, a position she held from 2003 until her retirement in 2015.

While this book narrates deep lows of professional maltreatments and blatant bigotry, financial hardships, and periods of loneliness, it also recounts the loud highs of promotions, recognitions and awards, wealth, worldwide travels, numerous blessings, tremendous joy, and fulfillment. Adding to the thrill is Moji's devotion to appreciating every individual who played a role, no matter how insignificant, in her success story. These range from the cab driver who offered her a life-saving ride upon her arrival at the Calgary airport when she was inadequately dressed for winter in February of 1978, to a mentor for whom she currently undertakes Betty's Walk for ALS (Lou Gehrig's disease).

This book provides a rare opportunity to learn from Moji's life story and accomplishments – an immigrant professional in the youth correctional system for 31 years, a wife, a mother of three children and a grandmother, a mentor, a coach, a professional model, and a community activist. From augmenting provincial youth correctional policies and founding many community groups that support and inspire women, children, and youth, to promoting education in diversity and cultural awareness, providing life skills programs for preteens,

teens, and parents, mentoring newcomers, and liaising between visible minority communities and the Calgary Police Services, Moji has done it all!

Read on and experience, as I have, a new sense of pride and belief in yourself, an overwhelming drive to succeed, and a keen motivation to make a difference in the world. More importantly, you will be inspired far beyond your dreams, learn how to turn challenges into opportunities for advancement, and learn how to take risks and dare to be positively different!

This is a unique story that needs to be read and shared far and wide. It is a great manual for many aspects of every individual's life journey. It is a book I will always keep close as a very useful guide for my own journey as a young, immigrant wife and mother in the legal profession.

Dr. Chidinma B. Thompson
Barrister and Solicitor
Calgary, Alberta, Canada

Table of Contents

Introduction

This book has been in the works for many years. Yet, it has not come to pass because I had a vision about writing a book. Candidly speaking, the thought of putting my story down on paper was the result of suggestion. I have been told many times over by many different people from many walks of life that I needed to write a book. Some of these people were immigrants like me who came to Canada later than I did. Others were Canadian-born individuals with immigrant parents. Still others were just regular folks who have been fascinated with and inspired by my story. All have shared one thought in common: my story is worth sharing. These people were the ones who encouraged me to write this book.

Despite the encouragement from others, I still didn't think my story warranted a book. It wasn't that unique from any other immigrant or anybody else for that matter. Then, some significant events happened to change my mind.

First of all, I became a grandmother ("Glamma") twice in one year, and third generation Canadians were born. Six months later, after over thirty years of civil service, I was faced with leaving my job with a severance payment or continuing to work under new working conditions that I did not agree with. I

1

pondered my options, taking time off to reflect on my life and my journey thus far, with my husband, children, and particularly, my grandchildren figuring prominently in the process.

I came to the conclusion that it was time to leave a legacy for my children and grandchildren by telling my story. My story is one of a hard-working, productive, intelligent, strong, kind, generous, proud, community activist, and black (oh yes, and beautiful!) African woman. Influenced by thoughts of my grandchildren, I decided that they needed a frame of reference as to their ancestors and where they come from, including grandparents and great grandparents. They needed to know about their roots.

. . . .

Born in Nigeria, I was raised in a large, loving, caring, but disciplined family. I am the seventh of eight children. I moved to Canada on my own when I was just 19 years old, one month shy of my twentieth birthday.

Neither my father nor mother were formally educated, but they were the two most resilient and smartest people I knew. They were both highly industrious. My mother, who was born in Lagos, Nigeria, ran a small convenience shop, sold anything and everything in its season, and managed the family finances.

From her, I learnt firsthand what it meant to have "multiple income streams". Meanwhile, my father, who was born in Cotonou (known then as Porto-Novo) in the Republic of Benin, which was a neighbouring, French country to Nigeria, was a bricklayer by trade. He was the foreman for many, major, construction projects in and around Lagos in the early days of mainland development. He was very successful at his trade, so successful that he purchased a parcel of land near one of his construction sites and became one of the first people to erect a two-story, concrete building at 90 Ikorodu Road, Fadeyi, Lagos. Ikorodu Road is a prominent road in Lagos state, being a major artery that connects Lagos state to the airport and all commercial focal points leading into and out of the state. Always hard working, my parents exemplified what it means to be diligent and productive in all that you do.

My mother, Munirat (Adelu) Balogun, was a beautiful, fashionable, petite, but fierce woman. She had a quick wit about her and possessed a love of dance. She was a strict, family disciplinarian but was also extremely kind and generous to extended family, neigh-bours, and people she didn't know. One of her many phrases to me was: "Common sense is one thing, education is another, but having both is essential in life."

My mother was especially caring towards children, never

wanting to see kids go hungry. As a Muslim, Friday was observed as a holy day with shops closed for afternoon prayers. After the prayers, my mother would put on a huge pot of tea and gather together sugar cubes and small loaves of bread, freshly baked and delivered from our neighbourhood bakery. Then, this bounty was distributed to all the neighbourhood kids who had lined up patiently with their cups. We, her children, were not allowed to have our own portion until the last child in line had been served. Her example was my foundation to selfless and random acts of kindness.

My father, Musediq Balogun, was a tall and handsome man who was gentle and equally as generous as my mother. I never saw him upset or argue openly with anyone...ever. His generosity was demonstrated during the Nigerian civil war of 1967 to 1970 when he harboured many of his Igbo (a cultural people of Nigeria) workers and tenants who chose not to leave Lagos for the Eastern part of Nigeria where the war was fought. A Frenchman with a knack for finer fashion, he loved his wristwatches, gold rings, and his customized, bejewelled shoes. Both my parents' generosity and sense of fashion had a profound impact on me.

I was especially close to my father who listened intently to all my plans, giving me much encouragement. He only had one request of me. He'd often say, "I want you to get an education." It didn't matter to him what I wanted to be, as long as it involved bettering myself through education. He was my hero.

Both my parents provided me with a solid grounding as to what it means to be vulnerable but strong, to be prudent yet fearless, and to be enriched by enriching others. I have been playfully teased as having my father's physique and my mother's tenacity with a sharp tongue.

There was and is a single conviction on which I have built my life. It was ever present as I grew up as a young girl and exists today in the strong and fulfilled woman that I am. That conviction is a sense of SERVICE, that is, the giving of myself – my talents, my time, and my resources – to others without expecting anything in return.

This foundation of SERVICE was also partly established by my classroom teacher, Mrs. McCauley. I remember in elementary school being called upon to write on the chalkboard for my classmates as she taught us. Along with teaching dependability, this exercise improved my penmanship and boosted my confidence in standing in front of a crowd and audience from an early age. Given additional responsibilities, I was relied upon to take inventory of the pens, pencils, erasers, and all other classroom supplies at the end of each school day. While this would have been perceived as a rather mundane task for some other students, I did not view it in this way. Instead, I was being trusted, relied upon by my teacher whom I looked up to and adored. Becoming reliable and dependable, honest and trustworthy under Mrs. McCauley's tutelage, I developed my strong sense of responsibility and SERVICE even more.

I arrived at my high school at the ripe age of 12 years old, settling in to my new school home where I would reside for the next five years. It was my first time ever being away from protective, older siblings. Even though I was somewhat shy, it did not take long before I volunteered as a junior house inspector for my dormitory. My job was to check and ensure that our house was cleaned and beds were made in military style. I was given the duty of making sure that my dorm mates and I passed the daily inspections, a responsibility I accepted graciously. You see, it made me happy to be trusted by my seniors while being responsible for my dorm mates. I worked hard with my classmates to make certain that our dorm met all the requirements, even lending a helping hand to younger students on chore and manual labour days. In addition, I joined the literary and debate team as well as the track and field team. By the time I was in my final year of high school, I was voted the senior prefect of my graduating class because of all my contributions. I was proud of my SERVICE.

Here are excerpts from two of the people that knew me from back then, both currently living worlds apart, yet expressing almost identical sentiments of their recollection of me. Their perspectives serve as an introduction of me to myself. I find it incredibly humbling to hear what these people thought of me at that young age.

"I grew up with Moji (Balogun) Taiwo, and we attended the same high school in Nigeria. She was the School Head Prefect during her final year in high school. We fondly called her "Mojee Balinga" because of her gorgeous "stepping" [style] with her big Afro hair. She was a fellow student that you could be proud of: very intelligent, trustworthy, dependable, dressed elegantly, and super neat.

"One thing I admired so much about her was her honesty. She would tell you the truth no matter how bitter

it was. I always expected her to support me whenever I did something wrong, but instead, she would firmly explain to me that what I did was wrong even though that was not the answer I was looking for. She was like the big sister I never had, but it took me a long time to realize that she truly loved me.

"Moji is someone that you can call upon anytime, and she will truly be there for you. I live in the United States, and she lives in Canada...and I still call her for advice whenever I need it even though we have been out of high school for over 40 years. I remember one of her most common pieces of advice when we were in high school was: 'Be honest in whatever you do, and do not be afraid to tell the truth no matter how bitter it is.'"

Jumoke Lawal

Sugarland, TX

"We used to call her by her nickname, Mojee Balinga. She was cheerful and a giver to all of the younger students. She took great pride in our dormitory cleanliness, gathering all of us together to clean as a team, showing us how elegant she was in all things."

Funmilayo Akanbi

Lagos, Nigeria

After a brief stint working for the Lagos State Department of Justice, Landlord, and Tenant Tribunal in Lagos, Nigeria, I embarked on a lifelong journey of education and human development in my new homeland of Canada. In both of my post-secondary institutions in Lethbridge, Alberta, I provided my services at will, from the Radio Booth upkeep to the yearbook committee. Being the only Nigerian student in the Radio Arts program did not deter me from getting involved in my school community.

In my city (Calgary) and work communities, I met other noble men and women of Nigerian heritage who also believed in SERVICE. Together, we have charted new territories and built legacies that future generations can build upon.

I grew up with a practise of sharing what I have, no matter how little it is. Therefore, it was no coincidence that my community involvements expanded when I moved to Canada. Canada, a nation built on values of respect, care, and sharing, presents many opportunities to contribute to the betterment of all. I have served and continue to serve with joy in many forms of community SERVICE be it home, school, work, neighbourhood, city, ethnic, and cultural communities, as well as the larger community.

Passionate about SERVICE, I look for the many opportunities to contribute to meaningful causes, acquire new knowledge, share my knowledge, and give back to individuals, groups, and communities. Primarily, I look forward to making a difference by contributing to peoples' lives in positive ways. Because of the early trust bestowed upon me and the special interest shown to me by my elementary school teacher, Mrs. McCauley, in addition to the care and example provided by my parents and an upbringing of sharing with my siblings and others, I have made it my mission to always be kind and generous with my time for all mankind, especially to young people.

As you can see, I feel a sense of great satisfaction when other people succeed. Going through life knowing that I have done my part in bringing about those successes, especially with my involvement in causes that positively impact individuals and the greater good of my community, brings me tremendous joy and fulfillment. I am truly blessed in blessing others.

What does this account of my background, influences, and motivations with relation to SERVICE mean for you? It means that it is not only the government, the rich, the people with no dependants, or people with lots of time on their hands who can make positive changes in their community or in other peoples' lives, but it also means that YOU can be a blessing with whatever you have wherever you are. The more you give (within your capabilities), the more you gain in life, as I have.

Aside from writing this book for the benefit of my offspring, I also hope that when you read through this book, that I – as a woman, an immigrant, a wife, a mother, a grandmother, and a service provider – will have inspired you to reach far beyond the stars, turning all your challenges into opportunities for advancement. It is my hope that my journey will empower you on your own journey to build a fruitful and fulfilling personal, emotional, professional, and prosperous life of SERVICE. My intention is that you will be able to identify your passion and find ways to have fun while using that passion to influence and uplift the people around you and in your communities.

A wish close to my heart is that my children, grandchildren, and future offspring will find courage, determination, and a resiliency to forge their own successful paths in life, paths guided by fairness and fearlessness, honesty and integrity, humanity and kindness. I extend this special wish to you, the reader, as well. This is your opportunity to become inspired, to apply the lessons and principles found in the accounts presented in this book to your own life. In turn, by sharing them with others, you can multiply your blessings because...

As we share, we teach.

As we teach, we learn.

As we learn, we grow.

To your fulfillment and contentment...

Moji Taiwo

Retired Civil Servant, Businesswoman, Community Activist, Speaker, Mentor, and Coach

Chapter 1

FIRST YEARS IN CANADA

Arrival

I arrived at the Calgary International Airport in Calgary, Alberta, on a cold, dreary afternoon in February 1978. Moments before landing, the captain had announced the temperature to be -27 degrees Celsius (-16 degrees Fahrenheit). Still, I did not fully grasp what that meant nor did I comprehend the extreme difference between that temperature and the +30 degrees Celsius (+80 degrees Fahrenheit) I had been enjoying a mere twenty-four hours earlier. As you can imagine, my face registered the complete shock of experiencing such frigid weather for the first time, and my body trembled when I saw the piles of snow, breathed in the thick, frozen air, and observed moisture clinging to the trees like glass crystals. It was a very cold welcome!

The officials at the airport greeted me with politeness, checked my documents, and ushered me through. Miraculously, it seemed, the door parted, and I found myself at the Arrivals reception area. I searched for the familiar face that was to have met me. After waiting for approximately one hour, my relative had not yet shown up, and I saw no one else that I could relate to. All the other passengers that had arrived on the same plane with me had dispersed. I began to panic quietly.

I had travelled with a few other black people during the first part of my journey from Lagos to London, England. However, once I boarded the British Airways flight from London to Calgary, I realized that I was the only black person on the aircraft. For some reason, I had convinced myself that, although I may have been the one, lonely, black person on the plane, I would soon see more faces that looked like mine when I landed. Upon arrival, I quickly scoured the faces around me...and I realized with some surprise that I was still the only black person in the sea of faces.

Other than when I was on the plane and engaged in speaking briefly with the flight attendants, I had never carried on a full conversation with a white person who spoke with such a different accent from mine before. It was a major adjustment to hear the English language spoken in an accent other than that which was common in Nigeria. Now that I had arrived in Canada with my thick accent, I quickly realized that I would have to alter my speech so that I could be understood, plus I would have to learn to understand the Canadian accent.

I instantly faced my first challenge as an immigrant in a new country – I needed to get to my destination. But first, I needed to figure out how to get there. The first person I approached for assistance on how to locate my brother, for that was who was supposed to have met me, did not understand my accent nor could I comprehend his. My panic increased. I felt cold yet sweaty all at the same time. I stepped aside, worked to regain my composure, gathered my courage, and then approached another person, a woman this time.

It seemed like this woman had travelled out of Canada before. I knew this because she was calm while listening and slow when speaking to me. She wanted to be sure we both understood each other. Next, she kindly directed me to the telephone booth, which I had never seen or used before, and told me that I could call the number I had with me. Here I was presented with my next challenge – I had not yet exchanged my money and did not have any Canadian currency for the telephone call. Fortunately, this kind woman gave me a quarter for the call, showed me how to insert the coin, waited for the beep, and then handed me the phone back and went on her merry way.

I made the call and was so happy to hear a voice at the other end! However, the voice did not belong to my brother, the person I most wished to speak to. I inquired anxiously if I could speak to Rafiu, my brother. Since he had not met me at the airport, I had assumed that he would be at home. The voice on the phone, which happened to be his mother-in-law, reported that he was *not* at home. Unfortunately, she was unable to inform me of his whereabouts or assure me that he would eventually meet me at the airport. This left me in quite the predicament.

Here I was, stranded in this strange and frigid new country. I had just finished travelling for over twenty-four hours in the air, had been at the Calgary International Airport for over two hours by this time, and I was cold, hungry, and exhausted. Something told me that I had to think fast to get myself out of the situation I was in. Asking for the address to my destination from the woman on the phone, I proceeded to go outside the airport to hail a taxi.

Here I was faced with my third challenge as a new immigrant – the climate. By then, it was late in the afternoon on that freezing, February day in Calgary. I did not know that the month of February was the heart of winter in this new land, and I had arrived in a skirted suit, open-toed shoes with no grips, and no winter coat. I was wholly and completely unprepared for the weather as I ventured outside into the extreme cold in an attempt to hail a cab.

I promptly dashed back into the airport and, with my teeth chattering, pondered what to do next. Then, a man approached and told me that he had seen me outside with my luggage and wondered if he could help me. He was not born in Canada, and he must have been an immigrant like me. I could tell from his accent, plus he had an olive-colored skin tone. Gratefully, I told him I was looking to hail a taxi and gave him the address of where I was going. It turned out that this man was a taxi driver. Gathering my luggage and noting the address, he told me to follow him to the taxi he had pulled up to the door. Shivering, I climbed inside.

He took me to my destination, but when I arrived there, nobody was home. At least, no one answered the door. I needed to make a decision quickly as the taxi driver was now beginning to have a concerned look on his face, although he was gracious throughout the whole process without complaint.

He suggested that I talk to the next-door neighbour. I scurried up the steps, still in my skirted suit and open-toed shoes, taking extra caution not to slip and fall as I almost had back at the airport, and knocked on the door. Using a doorbell was unfamiliar to me, for back in Nigeria, we didn't close the front door where I came from. Responding to my knock, a young, Asian lady with a newborn baby in her arms opened the door and instantly ushered me in before I could utter a single word. I suppose she must have known from observing my woefully inadequate attire that I was a new arrival, inexperienced in dealing with winters in Calgary.

After stepping into the warm, cozy, and well-decorated home, I told her that I was here to stay with her neighbour, and I provided my brother's name, which she confirmed was, indeed, her neighbour. I felt a huge wave of relief wash over me with that confirmation. I was not lost in this new country after all! Then, I told her that I needed to pay the cab driver but didn't have Canadian currency. Coming to my rescue yet again, she gave me the money to pay the driver, and he went on his way. I was so grateful for that kind man, and I am positive that he was especially sent my way to assist me with some of the challenges I encountered that day. My brother's neighbour was a blessing on my journey, too. She not only paid the taxi fare, but she welcomed me into her house, offered me a hot beverage, and kept me until somebody arrived at Rafiu's house next door. This was my first encounter with someone of Asian ethnicity, and it was very positive.

Rafiu arrived home late that evening and did not offer any explanation as to why he did not show up for me at the airport. I didn't bother to ask him either. However, I knew that I was on my own henceforth especially as it was not the only time he had failed to follow through on confirmed plans we had made. Unfortunately, this disappointment plus a few others immediately following my arrival clouded our relationship permanently.

The following day, Rafiu took me to the bank where I exchanged my Nigerian naira to Canadian dollars. Because Nigerian money had a higher value than the Canadian dollar at that time, I received a significant amount of money and subsequently opened a bank account with the Canadian Imperial Bank of Commerce (CIBC). After exchanging my money, I went over to the Asian lady's house (I am so sorry to have forgotten her name) to repay her for the taxi fare, but she refused to take it. Instead, she asked if I was all right and told me that, if I needed anything else, I should not hesitate to drop by her house.

Within one day of being in Canada, I had faced my share of obstacles. Yet, I had also met a few people who were kind and accommodating, helping me through those challenges. This was the beginning of my journey as an immigrant.

· ·

People have often asked me why I chose to move to Canada of all places, especially in the late seventies when I could have easily gone to anywhere in Europe instead. Most Africans tended to immigrate to England at that time. Being a single, black female, it was quite unorthodox to travel to this faraway "planet" called Canada.

The fact of the matter was that Canada had a shortage of manpower during this period of time and was looking for people to work (population in 1978 was approximately 24 million). The country had a need for workers in the trades and in domestic assistance. For myself, I was looking for an international education in broadcast journalism as well as a way to pay for it. With both Canada and Nigeria being members of the British Commonwealth of Nations, it made it possible for me to obtain a landed immigrant permit to work and study in Canada. While some people considered me to be a trailblazer, my thoughts towards myself were that I was either naïve or crazy – a girl who wasn't afraid of stepping into unfamiliar territory.

In those days, immigrants arrived through a variety of avenues. Some came as students with government scholarships, some arrived with British Commonwealth of Nations scholarships, some entered with visiting student visas or work visas, and still others came on a different mission with humanitarian visas. Canada has always opened her borders to immigrants, welcoming them with open arms, and most immigrants value the opportunities and generosity afforded to them. They adapt to their new country through their immense contributions to the betterment of the nation economically, politically, and culturally.

Getting Around and Finding a Job

In the week following my arrival, I realized that I was in the land of no return. There was no time to lounge around and acclimatize to the weather or the environment. I speedily learnt that if I wanted anything done, I must get up and get going quickly. There was no one to rely upon for long, as everyone had their own challenges and could only spare a moment of their time even if they had wanted to help. Instead, I needed to put in the effort myself to make things happen.

During this awakening period, I took inventory of my immediate needs. The first and foremost need was obvious — obtain appropriate winter clothing! If I didn't want to lose my limbs, this was my first priority. I had already felt a freezing, prickling sensation in my toes and fingertips the day of my arrival. To make matters worse, I cluelessly put my hands in warm water to try and defrost my poor fingers. The burning sensation I felt as a result was not funny! Next, I needed a Canadian piece of identification and a job. To obtain any of these necessities, I needed to find my way around the city.

Thankfully, Rafiu's wife, Genny, provided me with an oversized, winter jacket along with a pair of boots on loan, which were warm enough to get me to the bank to exchange my currency that second day. Bundled up in my borrowed attire with a bus pass in hand, I headed off to the mall to choose my own style of winter clothing that included toques, scarves, and different layers of gloves. I mistakenly thought that the more I piled on, the less chance the frigid, winter breeze could penetrate. I totally didn't consider that I needed room for blood circulation to combat the cold. I definitely was on a steep learning curve when it came to dressing properly for such cold weather.

I was now set to tackle the next item on my "to do" list – searching for a job. I had arrived with ample funds in employment savings from my job in Nigeria to sustain me for a few months, but a new reality was setting in faster than I had anticipated. You see, I had never paid rent before. I had left my family home where that had always been taken care of for me. Coming directly to Canada from my childhood home, I had no experience with this type of living expense. Therefore, paying rent and being responsible for my entire existence all by myself was a brand new venture.

Nevertheless, attending a boarding school for five years did help prepare me for taking care of myself to some extent. Planning ahead, I calculated my funds to see how long they would last in my new reality in Canada. As a result, I decided that the sooner I got a job the better!

I began to scour the employment opportunities pages in the local newspapers for any job that fit with what I was eligible to apply for. My visa allowed me to seek domestic employment meaning that I could apply for any cleaning job. As a new immigrant in those days, I wouldn't have had access to an office or better paying job anyway. Therefore, I was quite ready to accept any job that would provide me with money for my daily living expenses as well as some savings for my future education. My main goal now was not to deplete the funds I had brought with me.

After I had lined up a few places to go and submit applications, I mapped out the bus routes and the times it would take for me to get from point A to point B. That was actually the easiest part. Physically submitting applications in person was a process that was often discouraging, and particularly so when I could tell that the clerk was probably going to dismiss my application or even toss it in the garbage once I left. There were not many black people in the city back then, and the impression most white people held of blacks was from what was portrayed on television. As a black person, you were either considered a thug who was going to snatch their purses on the street or a baboon from Africa who lived in the trees among the apes. So, many Caucasians did not know what to do with those who originated from Africa and spoke British English, albeit with a thick accent.

The applications that ended up being dismissed or in the trash happened more times than I wish to remember. Yet, I never let this deter me, and I kept persevering in my quest. One side benefit I discovered through the process of dropping off applications throughout the city was that, by the time spring rolled around, I had become a master at getting around the city. This absolutely served me well.

One of Rafiu's friends, Joshua, also assisted me in my job search. Additionally, he helped me in the area of interview preparations. I was very grateful for this and all the small blessings I received along the way to finding a job.

I met a lot of different people on my various bus routes while job hunting. Some refused to sit with me, seemingly afraid that my black skin would rub off on them. Some stared at me suspiciously with fear on their faces and without uttering a word. Still others proved to be friendly, and I became acquainted with a few as well. It was a real mix of people in this new country.

In May 1978, I landed my first job in Canada working for a janitorial subcontractor cleaning a medical office building in downtown Calgary. It was a four-hour, evening job. I was assigned to a team of four that was responsible for the denture office floor. We were divided into two groups. One group took care of vacuuming, bathrooms, and garbages, while the other was responsible for dusting, sinks, and mopping. I was assigned the vacuuming the first day. You must understand that I had not used an industrial vacuum cleaner before. For me, it was an experience of a lifetime, that's how fascinating it was to be using such a wondrous machine. However, I was told that I was too slow for the time allotted. The second day, I received the sink cleaning assignment. It proved disastrous as well. These were not ordinary sinks with ordinary grime. They were metal sinks that needed to be freed of the denture-molding cast that had attached to them by the end of the workday. The particles needed to be pried and chipped from the sinks before I could wash and polish the sinks to their original, shining glory. I took my job seriously, and I meticulous polished all the sinks. Nevertheless, I was again too slow. My teammates tried to help me out but to no avail. By the time I arrived on the job the third day, I felt a sense of trepidation. That day, I was assigned to the bathrooms. Surprise, surprise! I was slow at this task too. I just couldn't seem to meet their timelines for completing these chores. Sensing that I was about to be fired, I called in the next day and quit. Personally, if I had been the employer whose profit margin depended on how many offices could be cleaned in what was (I felt) less than humanly possible in the way of time while only paying minimum wage, I would most certainly have fired me. To say the least, it was not the best start to working in Canada.

Back in Nigeria, I had successfully held an office job. Here, I was trading my expertise and experience for a cleaning job. This scenario was very common amongst early immigrants – a sacrifice made as a means to an end.

Most of the people in my circle at that time advised me not to quit that job because it could be quite difficult for immigrants to land jobs in the first place. Since most of them were in Canada on student visas and some even had young families, they didn't understand my boldness in quitting a job. Did I mention that I was being paid a mere $4.50 an hour? Anyhow, I appreciated their concerns, but I was determined to get another job where I wouldn't have to work faster than a machine and where my whole body wouldn't be sore from my head to my toes by the end of the shift. Also, I wanted a job where I wouldn't have to race to catch the bus only to miss it by a minute and subsequently have to stand in freezing weather at night for what seemed like an eternity while waiting for the next bus to arrive.

I continued to scour the newspapers for available work and talked to some other Nigerians and non-Nigerian immigrants I had met in the short month that I had been in the city. Funmi, a friend and one of the older women I had met, brought me a job application from the Calgary General Hospital's housekeeping department. Eagerly, I completed it and returned it through her. Within a few days, I was invited for an interview. Joshua gave me a ride to the interview…and I got the job! It came with better working conditions, better pay, and benefits. I was certain that the experience I gained from my brief, office-cleaning job was instrumental in securing this new job. Things were coming together.

Now that I had secured a job with more humane working conditions, my next goal was to upgrade my education to align with my future career plans. Therefore, I enrolled in evening English and Social Studies classes. If I was going to study broadcasting, I absolutely needed to know how English was spoken and written along with the history of Canada.

Having to work early hours for my job plus attending school well into the evening, I was on the bus for a fair amount of time each day and in the cold late at night. There was one particularly bitter cold and snowy morning that I will never forget...and do not wish upon anyone. It was 5:30 a.m., and I had walked about three blocks to get to the main road from where I lived to catch the bus for my 6:30 a.m. shift. It was extremely cold, snowy, and windy. I had been at the stop for about five minutes when my bus approached. I could not wait to step into the warmth and comfort of the bus! But alas, the bus drove right past me! The driver, I choose to believe, had not seen me standing by the shelter. Because it was a weekend morning, the next bus was not scheduled to arrive for another hour.

I returned home, frozen to my core. After taking a few minutes to thaw out my hands, I called into work and informed them that I was sick. This was one of the most trying and miserable days of my life as a young, single, female immigrant in a new country. I would have returned to Nigeria in a heartbeat that day had I possessed a return ticket.

Instead, I regrouped and weighed all my options...other than quitting that is. I knew I couldn't quit to escape everything unfavourable or unpleasant. Rather, I chose to move to the hospital residence.

This solution to my problem presented itself the day following my bus incident. I shared with a few of my co-workers what had happened and learnt that there was a bulletin board at the hospital's administration office with postings for accommodation and all sorts of other things for sale. Hopeful, I went to check out the board on my break and found a posting for the hospital residence.   The residence accommodated resident doctors, nurses, and other hospital employees. I was able to find a small room, complete with a semi-comfortable bed, a tiny closet, a wash sink, and access to a communal shower. I felt both relieved and satisfied.

This living arrangement ended up being perfect for me with many perks. First, I saved travel time to and from work, which also allowed me to sleep in a few extra minutes. I ate at the hospital cafeteria most of the time, reducing my grocery costs. The hospital was closer to my evening school than where I used to live, and therefore, my exposure to the winter elements was also significantly reduced.   I was quite pleased with my new arrangements.

Above all, I got to make my own decisions and create my own experiences, free of the influences of some of my earlier contacts. While I appreciated their concerns for me, I found the pressure of their opinions and advice to be limiting and restricting. I needed freedom to spread my wings and never lose sight of my goals in this new country.

By the summer of 1978, six months after my arrival in Canada, I had learnt to drive, got my driver's license, and bought a car. It was a 1973, two-door, mustard-coloured, Pontiac Astra. I paid $800.00 for it. I was more than happy with my new ride and eagerly looked forward to exploring the city on my own.

Summer Fun

That first summer, I purchased a flight ticket and travelled to South Bend, Indiana, in the United States to visit one of my older brothers, Kunle, whom I had not seen for almost ten years. I had a great time in the two weeks I was there.

That trip was just one part of my fun-filled summer. Upon my return to Canada, I attended many house parties, went dancing at nightclubs, met more people, and created new friendships. This memorable summer almost totally compensated for my first – and miserable – Canadian winter.

Now, my circle and I often just crashed parties, for there was no need to know the host to attend. Most international students who were attending higher institutions within the province converged on the nearest big city once classes ended in April. The ones on scholarships partied hard, and the self-sponsored students (like myself) collaborated and found ways to work and raise tuition fees for the following school year while enjoying the lavish parties of the government-sponsored students. There were students from African countries as well as the Caribbean Islands who could relate to being poor, struggling immigrants with no family support. Looking out for one another, some of us went on to forge lifelong friendships.

A New Partnership

At one of those house parties, I "unknowingly" met a poor, coy, caring, thoughtful, honest, funny, and handsome guy with a huge smile of pearly, white teeth that would have made a lot of money for Colgate. I say I met Aderinola (Derin) Taiwo unknowingly because I did not really notice him at the basement party hosted by one of the students in the city at the time. I was busy dancing the night away having fun as usual.

Derin called me the following day, but I didn't recall who he was. He described himself endlessly, but I still didn't remember him. Eventually, he asked if I would meet with him, as he was sure I would recognize him then.

I reluctantly accepted his invitation and met him during that week. As a precaution, I insisted that our meeting had to be during the daylight hours in a place that was familiar to me. Therefore, I told him to meet me at the end of my morning shift at the hospital where I worked. He agreed.

After meeting up with him, I vaguely remembered him from the party. He hadn't interacted much, but I recollected that he seemed to be people watching that night. Obviously, he had noticed me!

We clicked that day and began dating, as we both appeared to share similar goals and aspirations. Derin was quite a bit older than me, but, regardless of how young I was in comparison, he quickly realized that I was fiercely independent and undeniably focused. Some of the things I aspired to accomplish he had not seen other single, female, immigrant women take on before. He was intrigued.

We were together throughout the summer, but before he returned to school in September, he decided that our relationship was strong enough that he wanted to get married. This came as a total surprise to me, and thus I wasn't too sure of his proposal, mainly because I had never thought of myself as the marrying type before. Quite frankly, marriage was the last thing on my mind.

I shared my doubts with Derin. We engaged in many, long, heart-to-heart discussions about the matter. Finally, my doubts faded away, and I consented to become his wife.

Derin became my life partner on January 5th, 1979. After his proposal in the fall, he went back to school in southern Alberta, and upon his return to Calgary over the Christmas break, we got married. In the presence of a justice of the peace, we were joined together as husband and wife at the apartment of our friends, Tony and Iyabo Akintunde, who served as our witnesses. There were a total of five people at our wedding.

After the short ceremony, we ate a home-cooked dinner, cut a Safeway-made cake for dessert, and visited for the day. I was dressed in a beautiful, lilac-colored dress that I'd purchased at Reitman's, and my plastic bouquet of flowers was compliments of our host. Later that evening, my new husband returned to school in Lethbridge – over two hours away – and I returned to my residence at the Calgary General Hospital. That was how we spent our first night as husband and wife. I have always embraced my unorthodox ways of approaching and living life, for I am uniquely created! Naturally, my wedding was no different.

Our marriage ceremony was unconventional, but more so because, in the Yoruba culture of Nigeria where we both originated from, it would have taken a year or more to plan and execute our nuptials. Although there have been some modifications to the traditional practices in recent  years, when I got married almost forty years ago, all the long-time, formal traditions would have been strictly observed. The whole process is consistent among the Yorubas with minor details being different depending on the exact region(s) where the bride and groom come from.

To start with, traditional introductions take place. First, there would be an informal introduction of both the bride and groom to each other's respective, lower-ranking, family members – that is, the siblings. Next, this meeting would be followed by informal introductions to each other's higher-ranking, family members – particularly the mothers. Once these members were satisfied with the relationship moving forward, the mothers would orchestrate the next step – having the two families come all together in an official meeting.

Prior to this special meeting though, the bride's family would have generated a list of goods ranging from dry food items (including salt and sugar), cooking oil, kola nuts, both cloth and clothing, money, a Bible/Qur'an, and other important items for the groom's family to bring as dowry – the bride's price. Both families would choose a chairwoman who would negotiate this dowry fiercely (in fun) on their behalf. These negotiations would go back and forth until an agreement was reached between the two families. Neither the bride nor the groom would have a say in this process.

Once the offer to the bride's family was considered satisfactory and subsequently accepted, the official engagement could take place. This would be carried out as a formal celebration and be hosted by the bride's family. There would be plenty of food and drink and the bride's higher-ranking, family members would be primed and ready to receive all the representatives from the groom's family. In contrast with the typical, North American engagement party, this celebration would be rich with symbolism that represented long-held Nigerian traditions.

To begin the festivities, a veiled bride-to-be is escorted into the room to the sound of music by her friends and led down the centre of the room by the chairwoman to come before her parents who are waiting for her in a place of honour at the front of the room. There, she kneels before them for prayers. She is not released to join the groom's side until different envelopes stuffed with money from the groom's family have been presented to the higher-ranking representatives of her family. After the bride's representatives are satisfied with the exchange, the bride is then handed over to the groom's parents for prayers. At the end of these important, ceremonial steps, the bulk of the food gifts and money received from the groom's family as dowry are distributed amongst the women who have married into the bride's family, and the non-perishable gifts are packed for the bride-to-be.

Once the two families have agreed to become one through their children's union and it is sealed with these important traditions, then there is the proposal stage of the ceremony. A proposal letter from the groom's family is read out loud by the youngest member of the bride's family. In response, the bride's family presents an acceptance letter to the groom's family. Finally, an engagement ring is produced and given to the bride by the groom in the presence of all their family members as witnesses.

After all this formality, a wedding date is set...and the rigorous planning for the special day begins. Nigerian weddings are flamboyant, exuberant, expensive, much enjoyed by guests, and extremely time consuming. The mothers of the bride and groom spearhead the organization of the food, venue, entertainment, and the Aso-Ebi or uniform dress, which is worn as a sign of solidarity and unity at celebrations. For example, on the bride's side, their traditional Aso-Ebi may be made up of different shades of yellow, while on the groom's side, it may be different shades of green, and so it goes on. This takes some truly coordinated efforts by both parties to unify the two sides, coming up with a uniform that represents both families.

This planning period is also a time when the characters and personalities of the family members are tested. Most brides and grooms eventually get to have their special day and make it to the altar. Unfortunately though, there have been times when infighting and the desire for control within and between the families have derailed what was supposed to be a special and culminating moment for the new couple.

Although cultural practices are very much a part of my heritage, my husband and I chose not to go through all the formal ceremonies as per tradition...and I honestly didn't miss it. However, my mother did feel robbed of the planning and pleasure of putting on a full Nigerian wedding, whereas my husband's parents felt relieved.

Truthfully, I didn't miss the elaborate wedding ceremony because, as a young girl, I did not dream of getting married, nor did I fantasize about having the so-called "fairytale wedding" most girls dream of. Rather, my focus was on how I was going to make a difference in my lifetime. Meeting a wonderful man who supported my goals and independence and getting married to him was – and still is – a bonus for me.

Two years after my marriage, I finally got around to informing my parents that I was married. Of course, there was pressure on my mother's part to "right the wrong" as well as a hint of disappointment in my mother's tone. My bypassing all the pomp and ceremony of the typical Nigerian nuptials certainly wasn't her favourite piece of news. Yet, there was one part of our announcement that softened the blow.

My husband and I telegraphed our parents (no phones at our parents' houses) to announce the arrival of our first child and seized this joyous event as the opportunity to reveal that we were also married before they started to assume that we had birthed a child out of wedlock. Both sides of the family were overjoyed at the birth of a grandbaby! They eagerly supplied us with a list of names to choose from for our new baby. (It is traditional in the Nigerian culture for each set of grandparents to give names to the newborn.) My husband and I figured we had weathered the storm of announcing our unconventional wedding well.

However, just when we thought the dust had settled over the nontraditional marriage issue, my mother sent us a lengthy letter informing my husband and I that we must travel to Nigeria to have a "proper" wedding. Furthermore, she'd sent a copy of the same letter to my in-laws. She obviously had no concept of what it meant to be poor, struggling students in a new country with a brand new child! Where was the time to travel overseas with our school and work schedules? In addition, school holidays were spent working as many hours as possible to save up enough money for the next school year's fees and other living costs. My husband's parents were content not to have us come to Nigeria – quite frankly, it saved them a bundle of money – whereas my mother felt cheated because she couldn't showcase her daughter – the pride of any dedicated, Nigerian mother. The negotiations back and forth went on for several months. Finally, all parties eventually agreed to meet and conduct the traditional marriage ceremony on a much, much smaller scale in our absence. We received their blessings and moved on with our lives to our happily ever after.

. . . .

In 2004, we celebrated our 25th marriage anniversary in grand style with a vow renewal ceremony in the presence of our grown children and more than two hundred and fifty of our closest friends and family members from far and wide, including Nigeria, England, and the United States. It was a festival of sorts, with plenty of food, drinks, and the get-down, kind of dancing reminiscent of the moment my husband and I met each other...on the dance floor. I am looking forward to our 40th anniversary celebration coming soon!

Chapter 2

FORMAL EDUCATION

In the fall of 1978, I enrolled in the Western Canada High School adult education program to upgrade my English. I needed to meet the verbal and written prerequisites for admission into the Journalism program at the Southern Alberta Institute of Technology (SAIT). Sometimes, one must "go back" in order to regroup to move forward. Going back to high school was my way forward.

In January 1979, I enrolled at the same school for a social studies class. In this course, I learnt about the history and politics of Canada. Through this class, I developed a greater appreciation for the country, the people, and its democracy.

While attending these classes, I continued working at the General Hospital. I was still residing at the students' residence, saving my money for my future, and expanding my circle of friends. Many in my circle were immigrants from different countries and diverse cultural backgrounds, all sharing the common goal of maximizing their opportunities in this new country, regardless of whether we were, temporarily or otherwise, calling Canada home.

By spring 1979, I had finished my classes and applied to the Journalism program at SAIT. I was encouraged not to put all my eggs in one basket and to apply elsewhere as well. Although my preference was to stay in Calgary so that I could continue to work while I attended school, I grudgingly applied to Lethbridge Community College (LCC) as well.

SAIT's admission process was two-fold: the written plus the oral interview. I wrote my written test and passed. Therefore, I was invited for the oral interview. I was excited! I was on the road to achieving the next goal on my list.

I remember the interview vividly. One of the panel members was a prominent CTV Calgary anchorman who had retired recently but still produced special segments for the network. From my perspective, the interview went well. I get a special feeling in my gut when I know that I have done something well, and I had "that feeling" after the interview.

Approximately two weeks later, I received a letter notifying me that I was *not* granted admission into the program. Why? It was all due to my accent. Yes, in those days, you could be openly discriminated against without repercussion, or at least without a second thought. Furthermore, it didn't help that there was no education readily available about one's rights either. In response, I did do one thing within my control and rights though. I stopped watching the news anchored by that CTV anchorman.

You have to understand, I had been told that if I wanted to stay in Calgary and attend SAIT or any other institution in Calgary, there were programs that were accessible to immigrants like me...and broadcast journalism was not one of them. This field was apparently reserved for the elites. Nevertheless, I was not going to be deterred by that in any way. Instead, I was going to venture into that territory despite the naysayers and find a way for myself.

I discovered that the people in charge of the communications courses at SAIT during that time were not as progressive as I was in my thinking. I knew that my passion and drive would make me an excellent candidate for the Journalism program. Being an immigrant with an accent had nothing to do with it.

I wasn't just discouraged in my journalism pursuit by some of my friends at the university. In fact, a few of my contacts who were more mature and experienced immigrants had advised me, that as a female, I would be better off to take cooking or classes in the culinary line. They wanted me to go into a trade/career where I could easily get a job upon completion of the program.

Although they cared about me and were looking out for me, they forgot that they were not going to live my life for me. Besides, they had no idea how ill inclined and ill equipped I was to take on a culinary career. Even though I had grown up at a boarding school where independence and being able to fend for myself was taught, it did not, however, extend to cooking. Instead, we had cooks and house parents who prepared our meals. All we had to do was show up at the dining room where we were served. As a result, I never developed a love or inclination to cook. So for someone who did not enjoy cooking, how in the world could I have made a career of it? I cooked only because I had to eat, and later in life, I did it because my children needed nutritious meals, and I didn't want my family to starve. I was not about to commit my life to something I had no passion for.

Naturally, I was very disappointed when I was not granted admission into SAIT, but my hopes were not dashed. I was still waiting to hear from the college in Lethbridge. A short time later, I received a congratulatory letter of admission from Lethbridge Community College. I had been admitted into the Radio Arts and Journalism program. I was elated! My dream was taking shape!

I worked hard through the summer months, taking many overtime shifts and working weekend day shifts as my Saturday evenings were reserved for leisure activities. My goal was to save up enough money for the first-year tuition fee at LCC, accommodation, and food. I also had my car expenses such as gas, insurance, and minor maintenance to cover. With this plan in place, I diligently prepared for college in the fall.

In September 1979, I sold my beloved car, loaded everything I owned into my husband's car, which wasn't much, and we both headed for Lethbridge. Our first residence as a couple was located in the University of Lethbridge's student housing where my husband was enrolled. I settled into our temporary digs, and classes began.

The University of Lethbridge was on the west side of the city, and every day, my husband drove me to the community college on the south side of the city. We'd decided before school started that it would be much more economical for us to have only one vehicle. As my classes started earlier than my husband's and ended later, he could chaperone me to and from school, so this arrangement worked quite well.

All first-year, Communication Arts students attended classes together until the second semester, when we chose our specific line of study. I was thrilled to choose Radio Arts. I absolutely loved the storytelling aspects of the program along with the public speaking. I equally relished the interviewing process to get to the core of a story. Through interviews, I learnt more about the political structure of Canada and the humanitarian composition of its people. I also thoroughly enjoyed the radio booth and being able to have first access to all the new song releases hitting the airwaves.

The college environment was unique and intimate. Our student body was comprised of selected students from all over

Canada, including Ontario, Nova Scotia, Manitoba, Saskatchewan (Moose Jaw), British Columbia, and, of course, Alberta (Calgary, Medicine Hat, Red Deer, High Prairie, and other places). Carol Thibeaux was our copywriting teacher, our surrogate big sister, and a caretaker in the department. In addition, I developed a mentorship/coach relationship with the Radio Arts Program Manager, Mr. Ian Mandin (RIP). Mr. Mandin was a very patient, caring, and witty instructor. He infused humour and laughter into all his lessons, making his classes both fun and memorable. I was the only and first black student in the program and was treated like an African princess.

It was in this intimate setting that I met a young, smart girl named Connie Watson from a farm in northern Alberta who became my best friend. Through Connie, I gained knowledge about farming life and rodeo. She taught me how to improve my typing which was a mandatory course for the program. Later, she even crocheted a beautiful, baby blanket for my first daughter that has now been passed on to her own son, my first grandson. I am so thankful for this friendship and others that came out of my experience in the Radio Arts program.

The school year progressed, and life appeared to have settled into a comfortable pattern. My routine was well established and consisted of attending classes, going to the library, coming home late at night, and heading to bed to catch some sleep. The following day, the cycle continued.

Derin and I moved to an apartment off campus on December 1st of my first year in school. This set the scene for the first, major disruption in our married lives, an occurrence that was incredibly disturbing. It started when my husband and I noticed that our small apartment located on the top level of an old house on the south side of Lethbridge was often very cold at night. It hadn't been cold like that before. Naturally, we figured it must be due to the gradual arrival of winter...but the reason proved much more disturbing.

Instead, we found out that the landlady had deliberately turned off the heat to our unit due to pressure from her neighbours. They objected to her renting to a black couple even though we were rarely home, never caused any problems, and aspired to be successful and contributing citizens. We were, in fact, model tenants. However, in their prejudice against us because of our skin colour and their distorted perceptions of black people, our neighbours had mounted pressure upon her to get rid of us. We attempted to reason with her...but to no avail. She only responded by saying that, if we didn't like it, we should move. This made no sense whatsoever, especially since we had paid for the entire month of December and she didn't offer a refund. We were so gullible!

I called the police because we had not done anything wrong and knew that we had rights. When the officer arrived, he spoke to the landlady first and then came to talk to us. We were flabbergasted by his position. Not only did he not want to hear our side of the story, he basically repeated what the landlady told us previously. "You can move if you don't like it," was his final comment.

The whole experience was extremely unsettling for me! From that day on, I made it a personal mission of mine to become knowledgeable about the law, learning about all my rights and responsibilities as a citizen. I did not want to be caught in a situation like that again!

My husband and I moved in the middle of December without getting any refund from the landlady. On top of that, we had to shell out extra money to secure a new place. As a result, our budget had to be seriously recalculated. Although this was a hardship and made for a challenging time, it solidified a fundamental principle within me that fairness and kindness must play a larger role in my life. Years, later, this principle motivated both my husband and I to start a business in real estate, becoming the type of landlords that this landlady was absolutely not.

Thankfully, we found another place to rent, this time a sizeable basement suite with all the basic amenities we needed to survive. The landlord lived upstairs with his family. Both he and his wife were schoolteachers, and they had both a son and a daughter. We were blessed in that they were very nice and welcoming people, encouraging us with regard to our education. We breathed a huge sigh of relief.

Our distress from coming face-to-face with outright discrimination did not hinder us from moving forward with life. Our misfortune opened up the opportunity to, not just be more aware of our rights and to exhibit fairness and kindness to those in our path, it also opened the door to meet people who were *not* prejudiced towards people of colour. Opportunities can be found even in the hardships of life. This one led to finding a place where the neighbours were accepting, friendly, and giving.

We soon met an elderly neighbor named Thelma. Thelma was in her late seventies. She took an interest in us, bringing us baked cookies and cakes. She also gave us fruits and vegetables from her garden at the end of the summer. Living alone, Thelma received very few visitors. Wanting to give back, I began to visit with her occasionally as time permitted due to my school schedule and moved to more regular visits during the summer when I came home from Calgary.

I returned to Calgary at the end of April after my first year, resuming my summer job placement at the General Hospital where I had worked before. I was so fortunate in that they had told me to come back to work there anytime I needed to. It's always good to work hard and leave a positive impression when afforded the opportunity to do so. One never, ever knows what the future holds, and the positive impression you leave with people with regard to work ethic and attitude can open doors for you in the future. I must have left a positive impression with them and was thankful to have the invite to return.

I continued to work my regular shift from before as well as some overtime shifts in order to raise tuition and living expenses for the following school year. Derin and I also took an evening cleaning job during the ten days of Stampede at the Crossroads Hotel in Calgary to maximize our summer savings. After working during the day at the hospital, my husband and I traveled to the hotel in the evenings and worked until midnight. Being exhausted was an understatement, but I had a goal and was bound and determined to achieve that goal.

Once the ten days of Stampede were over, my normal work routine resumed. Yet, I was still exhausted. I had gone from someone who operated easily on five hours of sleep to being extremely lethargic, barely being able to keep my eyes open during the day. Concerned, I went to the doctor to have myself examined...and was notified that I was pregnant.

I couldn't believe I was pregnant! I insisted as such to the doctor, explaining that I was on birth control pills, had been on them for two years, and had gotten my period regularly. Moving past my protests, the doctor patiently explained that what I thought was my period was blood spotting, which was not a good sign. He recommended that I stop whatever physical work I was doing immediately.

Derin and I had kept our basement suite back in Lethbridge even though we planned to stay in Calgary over the summer. However, with the doctor's order, we both left our jobs in Calgary at the end of July and returned to Lethbridge. It was a huge blessing that we had kept the basement suite. Although jobless, we at least had a place to come home to for the time being.

We drove the two-and-a-half hours from Calgary to Lethbridge, pondering what lied ahead of us. Of course, my husband didn't want me to worry, but I could tell that he was concerned about our situation. Our lives had just taken a major detour, and our future seemed very uncertain.

We arrived home, emptied our car, and hauled our belongings into the suite when I noticed that our telephone answering machine was blinking with messages. Pressing the button, I listened intently. There were three messages, played one after the other. All three messages were job offers resulting from interviews we had gone through during the school season.

It was too late in the day to follow up with these calls, so we waited nervously through the night and prayed that the jobs were still available. To be honest, we didn't sleep that night at all. Our minds were filled with the fact that we had two school fees that needed to be paid, living expenses to pay, and now a baby to prepare for. It was a stressful and frightful time!

Eventually, the long night ended and morning arrived. One of the job offers had come from a meat packing plant. Calling them back, we fortunately discovered that the position was still available for my husband. Gratefully, he began training the following day.

Next, we called back the contractor who had offered a job in janitorial services. That job, too, was still available. It consisted of cleaning the office and bathrooms for General Foods in the evening, and they required us as a couple to fill the position. My husband was not exactly thrilled about me doing this job with him because of the doctor's order due to my initial spotting. However, I convinced him that I would be able to get enough rest during the day while he worked at the meat packing plant, and then we would be able to do the cleaning job together in the evening from six to nine with ease and not too much stress on my body. With these arrangements made, I did not pursue the third employment message left for us on the machine.

Despite the challenges and changes to our plans along with our future uncertainties, the summer of 1980 was a productive one. During the day, part of my resting period included morning visits with Thelma, my elderly neighbour. We developed a wonderful relationship, and she became a surrogate grandmother to my child when she was born. Graciously, Thelma taught me how to crochet and attempted to teach me how to knit. I became quite proficient at crocheting, but I could not for the life of me figure out the knitting. In addition, I learnt the "how to's" of both flower and vegetable gardening. I grew tomatoes, onions, potatoes, zucchini, lettuce, and carrots. Once my husband arrived home, it would be time for dinner, and then off we would go to the cleaning job. He was already exhausted from his day job, after which he had to soak his hands in warm, salted water to ease the swelling from working in the freezers at the meat packing plant. We pushed ourselves as much as we could and did what was necessary to adjust to this change in our plans.

The end of summer came, and we both returned to school full-time. Our plan was to keep the evening cleaning job until as close to my delivery due date as possible. However, due to early signs of labor and feeling more fatigued as time went by, it was harder and harder for me to keep up. Therefore, when we went to the job, my husband cleaned both the male and female bathrooms because I had to sit periodically to rest. Somehow, though, the contractor who hired us became aware of this through some of the General Foods plant workers and gave us an ultimatum. We both had to do the job together...or else.

By the last week of January, I began to experience more cramps and false labor but continued to push through the cleaning job. One evening during work, a male employee at the plant, who had often joked with us when we were there, noticed that I wasn't feeling well and summoned my husband to attend to me. He encouraged us to leave the job, as it was not worth the risk of a possible medical emergency. We quit the job that night, and Governor, as we affectionately called this man, became our friend.

We often visited with Governor's family, and they visited with us in turn throughout our stay in Lethbridge. He was an avid hunter who shared his deer and moose meat with us. In addition, He was also a skilled, wood craftsman. He presented us with a beautiful wooden clock with our baby's picture on it as a gift. It's been over thirty-five years, and that clock still hangs on our mantle today. Just when we were experiencing stresses in our lives, we were blessed with the Governor's friendship, which relieved some of the strain we were under.

In September of 1980, the second year and third semester of my Radio Arts program began. As I sailed through it, my belly grew steadily. My program mates and faculty showered me with much care and attention. They even got me a couch to lie on whenever I felt tired. They were so kind, and I was so very grateful to them.

The fall semester concluded, and I started my last semester at LCC. It looked like I was going to be able to push ahead and deliver the baby close to graduation; at least, that was my wish. In spite of my wishes, the baby decided to make her appearance midway through my final semester. She arrived on February 6th, 1981, weighing in at 6 pounds (2.721 kilograms) after many false

54

labour trips to the hospital and calls to my doctor, Dr. Evelyn Harding. We named our firstborn Ololade, meaning "the keeper of wealth has arrived". Nicknamed Loly, she was the cutest little thing with her shiny, curly hair and long, curly eyelashes. Back then, there hadn't been many black babies delivered at the Lethbridge Regional Hospital. Consequently, my baby became the star of the nursery ward.

We returned home after one week in the hospital and began to bond as a family, albeit with many sleepless nights. Due to our inexperience and lack of family support, we were unprepared for dealing with a colicky baby. Loly cried a lot at night, but slept during the day while at daycare. The caregivers at the daycare loved her, not only because she was cute, but also because she slept most of the time making it easy to care for her. Meanwhile, we got no sleep at home at night.

After one month at home with my baby, I returned to classes in March and graduated with my program mates in April of 1981. This period was especially challenging for me, as you can imagine. Besides having a colicky newborn, I was juggling a full course load of classes, including an 8:00 a.m. commercial/creative writing class. If all this weren't enough, I had to dash across a major road from the college campus to the daycare in between classes to breastfeed my daughter. I was utterly exhausted most of the time, and to be honest, I don't know how I pulled through. But I did. I was very proud of myself for pushing though and graduating despite the challenges.

Based on a combination of my marks, a project I produced, and my personality, I was recommended to a radio station manager in Lethbridge for an internship opportunity. The manager at CJOC FM Lethbridge hired me, and I started there in early May of 1981.

A few dynamics were in place right away with this job. First of all, the camaraderie and intimacy that I had enjoyed at my college campus was absent. The station was run by family members of the owner, an owner who happened to own most, if not all, of the media outlets in Lethbridge. They had never seen nor worked with a black person with an accent before. I was definitely made to feel like an outsider. I also had a small baby who required standard medical checkups and care. Having to take time off to take my baby for medical appointments strained the placement further. I began to question if this was the place for me.

Although the manager who hired me understood my training schedule and the purpose of this internship, the people I was placed with had a different plan. I was relegated to doing menial jobs that had no relevance to my education and training. This internship was not working out as I had hoped.

Now, I'm a very intuitive person who is keenly aware of my surroundings and situations. By this time, I knew that I did not belong at CJOC. The environment was not conducive to my career advancement at all. Furthermore, I couldn't possibly apply to any other media outlets in the city because the same owner controlled them at that time. I could move to another market/city, but with a husband still in school in Lethbridge, moving was not an option for me. I now had a child, and moving back to Calgary for my old, guaranteed summer job at the General Hospital was also not practical. Therefore, I immediately applied to the University of Lethbridge and searched for another job for the summer.

While I waited to hear back from the University of Lethbridge about the status of my application, I took a retail job at the local Zellers. Mind you, I didn't tell them that I had just graduated from college. Otherwise, I probably wouldn't have gotten the job, as they were more interested in hiring employees less likely to leave in a few months. Keeping quiet about my future plans, I was hired as a cashier where my mandatory typing course in college was put to excellent use serving the customers faster than the others. They loved my friendliness with the shoppers and did not want me to leave at the end of summer. I had to tell them that returning to school had always been my plan.

By mid-summer, my admission letter arrived with a one-and-a-half year credit towards a four-year Bachelor of Sociology degree program. With my newfound realization that it wasn't only Calgary whose media personnel were closed-minded to having immigrants in their program, I came to the painful conclusion that Alberta was not ready for a radio announcer with a different accent. Thus, I reassessed my professional options and decided that I would enjoy the field of humanities and service, hence my enrollment in Sociology. Also, my husband's and my plan at that time was to return to Nigeria once my husband completed his graduate degree and where I could use my broadcasting training. In the meantime, I could compliment my education further by obtaining a humanities degree. It was a clever move on my part not to put my life on hold until our planned return to Nigeria, for my family and I never returned to Nigeria. Rather, we made Canada our permanent home.

I was elated when I received my admission to the university to pursue a sociology degree. However, it meant that I now had two-and-a-half more years of school to fund as well as a baby to care for. During that summer, I worked my cashier job with Zellers during the day, and Derin and I continued with another cleaning job we'd secured in the evening. We got this job when I returned to school in the fall of 1981 to raise money for our baby's needs. Our daughter went to daycare during the day,

58

and we took her with us to the cleaning job in the evening. My goal was set, and now I was doing my best along with my husband to meet that goal.

I knew I was going to be exceptionally busy in the coming months with school, so the summer was spent having as much fun as possible in between our work schedules and despite our financial circumstances. We travelled to places of interest that were close in proximity to the city as well as making a trip into the neighbouring province of British Colombia (BC). Enjoying these mini-holidays immensely, we visited national parks and historic sites such as Waterton Lakes National Park, the Frank Slide in Pincher Creek, Head-Smashed-In Buffalo Jump in Fort MacLeod, nearby Hutterite colonies, and Sparwood, BC. During this time, our family also moved to a two-bedroom apartment building on the south side of the city where little Loly finally got her own room.

The fall of 1981 arrived along with the next phase of my formal education. My studies in sociology began in earnest. The environment on campus was more open and expansive compared to the close-knit, college campus I was used to. Nevertheless, this did not overly intimidate me because, as my husband attended the university, we as a family often visited there to use the amenities, particularly the library. Thus, I was quite familiar with the landscape. Yet, I still had to adjust to attending my different classes in different areas of the campus.

My studies included courses in Anthropology, Canadian History, Geography and Population Distribution of Canada, Crime and Delinquency, Canadian Criminal Justice, Corrections, Juvenile Delinquency, and Psychology of Human Development, plus many sociological independent studies on Youth, Crimes, and Rehabilitation. It was at this junction that I decided that my passion for helping people, especially young people and people who are disadvantaged, would be my next career choice. I had always had a penchant for helping people since my elementary years and my high school, boarding school days. Coupled with my work with the Lagos State Ministry of Justice in Nigeria, I found myself coming full circle by combining my love of service, advocacy for fairness, and justice for all with this new career direction. My communication (Radio) arts training and public speaking experiences also served me well during my independent studies, presentations, and class debates.

With baby Loly in tow and always conscious of our expenses, I made the most of my tuition fees by taking the maximum number of courses allowed per semester. Back then, a full semester course load for a full-time student was three, but a maximum of five courses was permitted. Not only did I take the maximum course load in the fall and winter sessions, I registered and completed the maximum amount of classes in the spring and summer sessions as well. I was determined, and I was focused.

By the end of my first year at the university, my marks were excellent, allowing me to secure a marking assistant position. I marked year one students' exams and papers for professors in my faculty. It was a good paying job, and I was paid per paper. My husband had also landed a good paying job at the university by that time, too. Everything was lining up beautifully, I thought.

Then, I met two, adult education students in one of my classes...and my life got even better. Lynda Nichol and Gloria Skinner (Haddow) were older than I, and both had three children each. They had led interesting lives as youngsters and were now registered in the provincial government's adult education program. This program provided adults on government assistance the opportunity to enroll in post-secondary institutions to take grade twelve upgrade courses. This, in turn, led to a full, university degree program for each participant. Allowing these special students to reclaim and improve their lives through higher education, the program gave them the means to be positive role models for their children. These brave women wanted to break the cycle of abuse and poverty for the sake of their children through higher learning.

Lynda and Gloria were enrolled in the Faculty of Social Work. They both graduated and went on to have successful careers with the Government of Alberta as Social Workers. Gloria worked in Calgary as a manager with Alberta Child and Family Services. She truly cared about children and families and wanted to help them achieve a better life and home environment. We continued our sweet friendship until her passing in 2010, may her soul rest in peace! My dear friend Lynda still works as a Career and Employment Consultant with Alberta Works today.

On one of the many occasions that I sat with Lynda, Gloria, and Mitch (the refreshment machine caretaker whom Gloria introduced me to) at the student union lounge, a discussion ensued about children, schooling, and all other womanly responsibilities. They found out that I had a baby and that we traveled back and forth from the south side to the west side where the university is located at least three times a day. Next, the conversation led to our accommodation and the cost of it. These dear ladies were aghast to discover that we were paying way too much for our accommodation considering our income. Informing me about the city's low-income housing, they told me how I could apply for it. They also told me there was low-income housing located on the west side within walking distance from the university. I was thrilled and could hardly believe these angels that God had sent my way. I followed up on their leads, applied for the accommodation, and was approved. Two months later, we moved to a three-bedroom townhome on the west side of Lethbridge on McGill Boulevard.

Lynda and Gloria and I continued to hang out at school whenever possible, developing a family friendship outside of school as well. Lynda and Gloria loved to party and loved life. We all went to Mitch's house for holiday celebrations and to Lynda's for birthdays. They all came to our new house for Easter and other birthdays as well.

The school years rolled along, and so did my friendship with these lovely ladies, but I was especially close with Lynda. I am grateful that they came into our lives when they did, enriching it through friendship, care, and good times.

After much hard work, I went on to finish my degree coursework in the spring session of 1983. My degree was conferred in May 1984. It was a very proud moment!

Chapter 3

PREPARING FOR THE FUTURE

Our first daughter, Loly, was now a little over two years old. My husband was continuing his education through graduate studies in the United States. In preparing for his departure, it was in our plans to have another baby before he left. Needless to say, I was expecting a baby by the time I finished my university degree coursework, and my due date was to be late August to early September. This timeline was cutting things pretty close as my husband's classes resumed mid-September.

I committed the rest of that summer to preparing for the arrival of our new baby as well as spending quality time with my toddler. We spent a lot of time at the swimming pool and riding bicycle. In addition, we enjoyed countless hours at the local library that was in the same complex with the swimming pool. Since most of our waking hours since Loly's birth had been spent at the university library, she had developed an early love for books and reading. During this same time, I searched for jobs and dropped off resumes for employment openings where I could use my education.

Although we had a plan, nothing ever transpires exactly as you expect. The arrival of our second child definitely proved this. My husband's departure time for the United States came upon us much more quickly than anticipated...and yet the baby had not arrived. Once again, we both had a tough decision to make. He could stay home until the baby came and miss his graduate studies commencement date, or he could leave for school and miss the birth, leaving me to deal with both a newborn and a toddler by myself in those first weeks.

We deliberated back and forth. Weighing all our options, we considered both the pros and the cons of our pending decision. Finally, we both agreed that he should go on to school. As hard as it would be, I would do my best without him.

Derin left, driving from Lethbridge to Central Missouri State University, Missouri, U.S.A. He called us from a pay phone at every rest point along his way. (There were no personal cell phones at the time.) Then, he called to check on us from his campus the following day and every day until his return home at Christmas that year.

While I waited for the baby's arrival, I landed a job interview with a local community agency – Southern Alberta Community Living Association (SACLA). I attended the interview and did very well...but there was a problem. I was due to deliver any day by then. While I was discussing this matter with one of the interviewers, a lady came into the room. I don't know whether she was summoned because they had to make a decision, or whether she had seen me while I was in the waiting room.

Turning out to be an angel sent to my aid, she said to me, "We would like to offer you a weekend position after you have your baby and are ready to start work."

Doing a double take on my seat, I was left totally speechless! For a chatterbox like me who was (and is) rarely short for words, I was beside myself with astonishment and gratitude...but I couldn't utter the words. I later found out that my guardian angel – Heather was her name – was the Programs Director of the agency. She had no idea the gift she had just bestowed upon me with that job offer and the stress it lifted off my heart that day. Then again, maybe she did know. Maybe she was a mother, a fellow working mother who saw another woman desperate enough to apply for a job nine months pregnant and waddling into a job interview. Better yet, maybe she saw a determined woman who was willing to work hard for whatever she wanted. Whatever it was that she saw in me, I was extremely grateful to her for giving me a chance.

I ended up working at SACLA until my family and I relocated to Calgary. During that time, I discovered that Heather was a kind-hearted woman all around with a few adopted children of different races, one or two of them with special needs. It was a pleasure and honour to work with her.

With employment for the future settled, it was now time to have this baby. Before that could happen, arrangements for Loly needed to be made. Thankfully, I had made a paid, babysitting arrangement prior to my husband's departure with my next-door neighbour, Maggie, who lived at the same municipal housing complex we lived at.

Maggie and her family had fled the civil war in El Salvador. She lived with her mother, husband, and three young sons ranging in age from five to ten years old. They were very friendly and loving people. I had gotten to know the family better after I had completed my schooling and had some time to spare for Maggie. Maggie was enrolled in an ESL (English as a Second Language) class, and I helped her with her conversational English skills as she relayed her life story and how they escaped the war. Her war and escape tales gave me a better appreciation for human beings and humanity.

Ten days after my husband's departure for school, I started to have cramps, and the pain intensified very quickly. I knew what true labour pains were by now. Since I had packed the hospital bags a few weeks earlier along with a bag for Loly for her brief stay with Maggie, I was ready. My neighbour took Loly and her bag while I drove myself to the hospital. I had a direct line to my doctor, Dr. Evelyn Harding, whom I had contacted earlier in the day, and she instructed me to report to the hospital, and she would meet me there.

The labour intensified as I drove closer to the hospital. The closer I got, the farther the hospital seemed to be. The baby, who had taken its sweet time up until this point, was now ready to come…and she was checking in fast! I pulled up to the hospital door just long enough to park at the emergency entrance and waddle up to the admitting desk in severe pain. The rest was a miracle in the making. I was immediately placed on a stretcher and wheeled off to the delivery floor where Dr. Harding was already waiting. The baby arrived so quickly. It took just three hours from the initial onset of labour to delivery.

Our second daughter arrived at the Lethbridge Regional Hospital on September 30th at 11:13 in the morning and weighed in at 7 pounds even (3.175 kilograms). She was given the name of Adejoke, meaning "the crown will pamper this child". She was both healthy and beautiful!

By the way, a hospital attendant had to remove my car from the emergency entranceway to the patients' parking lot and bring in my hospital bag. It all happened so fast. What a service!

Unfortunately, com-plications set in during and after Adejoke's birth. During delivery, I lost a significant amount of blood and ended up requiring a blood trans-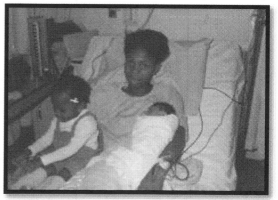fusion. While being transfused, I still continued to lose blood. Eventually, though, the blood flow was stabilized. Next, I developed a very high fever, which I later learnt was a sign of my body rejecting the foreign blood. I panicked! Here I was with a brand new baby in the hospital, my toddler was staying with my neighbour, and my husband was far away in a different country...and I could die if my body continued to reject the transfused blood. I felt so alone and scared!

Dr. Harding sprang into action! Providing me with anti-rejection medication, she reassured me that I would be all right. In the meantime, I was hot from the fever, but I was shivering uncontrollably with my teeth chattering loudly. The nurses surrounded me with basins of cold water and crushed ice with fans blowing over them directly at me in order to bring down my high temperature. It took a day or so before my fever subsided. I was very grateful for the great care the nurses gave me during that scary first day or two and for how they looked after my precious newborn while I recovered.

Finally, I began to feel well enough to see my new baby, who had been sent to the nursery for care while I was fighting the fever. Next, I received a visit from Maggie who brought Loly up to see me and meet her new baby sister. During my stay, she brought Loly to visit me at the hospital daily. Lynda, Gloria, and Mitch also came up to visit the baby and me during our hospital stay.

My newborn baby and I were released to go home after one week in hospital. I joyfully reunited with Loly and the comforts of our home. My older daughter was so happy to see us and was very helpful with her new baby sister. I was glad to be home!

The first few days went relatively smoothly. Then the reality of being alone with two babies along with the exhaustion set in. Maggie came by from time to time to help out, and I received nightly calls from my husband after the children had been fed, bathed, and put to bed. The calls were comforting, and I eagerly looked forward to them. Those first few weeks alone juggling the care of two very young children were a challenge, especially considering the extra tiredness I was under due to my delivery ordeal.

By late October, my father and younger sister arrived from Nigeria for a visit. This was a very welcome relief. They filled the void of adult conversations and loneliness, as well as assisted with general help around the house until my husband returned home for the Christmas break from school. Having missed her daddy, Loly was very excited to have him home again when he finally arrived. It was a touching moment, too, to have Adejoke and her

daddy meet for the first time. We were thrilled to be reunited as a family once again.

Aside from being happy to have my husband home, making Christmas celebrations special had become extremely important to both of us. Ever since the time our old landlady turned off the heater and we had to move in the middle of December, we were determined to turn what was a depressing moment and tainted holiday in our lives to a time of celebrating and sharing with others. Also, due to the loneliness of previous holidays with not having any family around to celebrate with, we desired to create more meaningful memories with others. In the past, we had spent most of the holiday season at the university library preparing for the winter semester while most students went home to their real or adopted families. Instead, from that moment on, we promised that we would always celebrate with other friends, including foreign students who may or may not have anywhere to go during the holidays. That year, we hosted our first Christmas gathering. We had an amazing party!

January 1984 came upon us quickly. It seemed like my husband had just returned home, and now he had to leave again. He returned to school, and my daughters and I were left to adjust to living day-by-day without him once more. The winter days were short with long nights. To keep ourselves busy, we spent most of our time at the library or walking the long hallways of the University of Lethbridge to pass the time.

One particular morning after I had put the girls down for their naps, I found myself sitting alone and pondering about my life and my future. I am not used to relaxing for too long, and being at home for three months by this time was more than enough for me. I was getting restless! Ready to make a change, I decided to contact Heather, the lady who had offered me a job at Southern Alberta Community Living Association (SACLA), to let her know that I was ready to report for duty. I was given a position as a weekend support worker with special needs adult men and women who lived semi-independently in adjoining duplex residences. My shift covered a forty-eight hour time period from Friday at 4:00 p.m. to Sunday at 4:00 p.m. where I had to sleep over on location in order to be available twenty-four seven. The job came with decent pay...at least much more than I had ever made up to that point. The investment on my degree was paying off, I thought to myself. Without hesitation, I accepted the offer and worried about the logistics of childcare for my babies later.

Now, Maggie and I had developed a very close relationship since the birth of my second daughter, Adejoke. Her care of Loly while I was in the hospital, and her assistance afterwards was a huge blessing in a time of need. She was compensated with nominal payments and help with her English lessons in the evenings. Her sons also came over to my house to play from time to time.

With my new job, Maggie factored in prominently into our lives. I arranged for her to care for my babies from Friday afternoon to Sunday afternoon while I went to work. In return, I tutored her in the evenings during the week. She was a godsend, and I appreciated her immensely. It worked out perfectly for us both, and our friendship continued for many years afterwards.

My friendship with Lynda, Gloria, and Mitch also continued. I often met up with them during the week at the student union lounge of the university where Mitch still took care of the snack bar machines. Gloria and Lynda were working on finishing up with their studies at that point.

During one of these social meetings in April of 1984, we were discussing our individual futures and employment prospects. Gloria had not secured a job yet after graduation and naturally wanted to leave Lethbridge for the bigger city of Calgary. I also knew that, for my family and me to reach our goals and full potential, we most likely would have to leave the constrictions and lack of opportunities in Lethbridge for educated immigrants for a larger city. Fortunately, Lynda was already employed while completing her degree. So, I was curious and wanted to know where she was working, how she got the job, and how she could assist me in my own employment search. Mind you, I still had my weekend support staff position at SACLA. While I appreciated and enjoyed the people around me at SACLA, I viewed the job as a stepping-stone to building my career. SACLA was the foundation to my resume.

I found out that Lynda had worked the previous year in a summer student, placement program while completing her degree, and she had returned to the same placement program for her graduating year. Upon graduation, she was retained and offered a permanent, full-time position. This meant that she had more degree-related, career experience than Gloria and I. I learnt an important lesson here, which I often share with immigrant parents and their young adult family members. I advise that it is advantageous to gain career experience(s) relating to one's degree while in school through co-ops, internships, and mentorship placements before completing one's education. These experiences on the resume highlight and complement the relevancy of one's education, making one more attractive to a potential employer after graduation.

I inquired how Lynda could assist me. She informed me that her office had just posted an advertisement for the Summer Temporary Employment Program, and they were looking for students who planned to return to school or who had recently completed their education. Jumping for joy at the news, I immediately scheduled a separate meeting with Lynda to find out details about the position, the deadline for submitting an application, and if possible, to whom I could speak to at her office in preparation for the interview, an interview that I had not been invited to yet. I couldn't believe the coincidence of my good fortune on a day that started with just a regular, casual meeting with a good friend.

Two days later, Lynda and I met and went over my resume and the position requirements as posted in the newspaper advertisement. They were looking for a counsellor for their Employment Opportunities Program. The successful candidate would work with adults on social assistance, assisting them with resume building, job searches, and program placements. I was certain I could do the job well, especially when it came to assisting and serving the public.

I completed my resume and attached it to the employment application Lynda had brought for me. As I wondered out loud about how I would be able to get a babysitter to watch my daughters so that I could go and submit my application, Lynda gave me another priceless gift. She casually announced, "Oh, no need to get a sitter. I already spoke to Stan, my manager, about you. I'll submit your application for you." I was dumbfounded! In those days, applications were delivered in person, as there was no Internet yet. I could never repay that girl for taking that extra step for me!

After Lynda submitted my application on my behalf, I was invited for an interview the following week. My philosophy was to never take anything for granted, especially an opportunity to use my education. Therefore, I prepared very well for that interview by researching the position, how my education was related to it, and what special skills I had to contribute to the position and their clients.

I felt extremely good about my interview, and I was sure a positive reference from Lynda helped with the impression I made, too. I got the job and commenced work two weeks later. I was so grateful to Lynda for all that she had done! Meeting her, Gloria, and Mitch has brought so much blessing to me and to my family.

Acquiring this job presented to me my next set of challenges. I had a toddler and a six-month-old baby that needed to be looked after. I still had the 48-hour, weekend, support job with SACLA, and now I had this offer of full-time work for the summer working for the Government of Alberta Monday to Friday, 8:30 a.m. to 4:30 p.m. Not only did I have to arrange for more stable childcare for my babies so that I could work Monday through Friday, I needed to decide whether to keep or leave my weekend job. However, these were positive challenges to have, and I was ecstatic about the opportunities ahead of me.

I called my husband to share the exciting news. He was very happy for me and for us. Immediately suggesting that I give notice of my intention to quit the weekend job, he expressed relief that I would no longer have to work on weekends away from home and our girls. Little did he know that I was quietly contemplating keeping both jobs for as long as I possibly could to build my resume. Plus, providing some extra cash flow for the family didn't hurt either. As a matter of fact, I couldn't remember the last time I held just a single job. As a student, when opportunities presented themselves to have two jobs and save money towards tuition, I always took it. In the same manner, I wasn't going to miss this opportunity to continue to save for my family. Therefore, I didn't immediately respond to my husband's suggestion to quit the weekend job. I merely focused my attention on getting my babies registered at a reputable daycare close to our home.

For the remainder of that week, my excitement built up as I researched, inspected, and subsequently found a good daycare on the west side of the city for my little ones. The daycare was close enough, as I could travel between our home and my new job within thirty minutes. Only after I confirmed all the logistics did I share my plans with my husband.

The plan was to work at my government job Monday through Thursday from 8:30 a.m. to 4:30 p.m. Then each Friday, I would take a half-hour lunch break rather than an hour, thereby allowing me to leave earlier at 4:00 p.m. to pick up my children from daycare. I had arranged all this with my direct supervisor when I went in to the office to complete my commencement papers. Of course, I didn't tell her that I needed that half hour because I was going to another job. That was an unnecessary detail that I did not volunteer.

I started my new job with the government in May 1984. The girls went to daycare during the day while I went to my day job. On Friday evenings, they went to Maggie's house until Sunday evening when I returned from my weekend, sleepover job. Life's schedule was very full!

With such a packed agenda, the days flew by quickly. Therefore, evening activities with my girls during the week were especially important. Sunday evenings I reserved for preparing for the following week. I maintained this strict and busy schedule until my husband completed his program and returned home at the end of June.

Both the girls and I were so happy to have him home! What a relief for all of us, too! The babies didn't have to go to Maggie's on the weekend any longer, but being next-door neighbours, we still got together on a regular basis. My husband could now provide assistance with the children and also with household chores. Phew! Did I say I was relieved?

It would have been very helpful had we been able to sponsor my mother, my mother-in-law, or another relative to come live with us and assist us with childcare. However, the Canadian Immigration Sponsorship Program was very stringent and onerous at the time. It was based on the family's combined income, and being as ours was on the lower end of the scale, we were too low to qualify.

Once I had a permanent, full-time job, both my husband and I applied to sponsor my niece. The process took approximately two years by the time she got to the final stage, which was the face-to-face, "personal suitability" interview stage. Unfortunately, she was disqualified because she did not know what a vacuum cleaner was nor had she ever used one before. Two years of anticipated relief and stability for our children vanished just like that...unless we wanted to appeal the decision, which would have cost us more time and money. There were no privately owned, certified, immigration agencies that provided services that could have assisted us either like there are today. Thus, we soldiered on, doing our best on our own.

I continued to work both jobs, gaining valuable experience, forging new friendships, and building reputable references that cemented the foundation of my career. Derin helped with the children while pursuing his own career opportunities. Our ultimate plan for the future was to move back to Nigeria, therefore we were open to relocation within Alberta and beyond if that was what it took to do so, and thus our employment searches were unlimited. Although I held two jobs, I never stopped scouting out better opportunities, nor did I stop applying for other positions.

During one of those searches, I came across a job posting for Youth Workers with the Government of Alberta under the Ministry of Justice and Solicitor General. The Federal Government of Canada had recently proclaimed a new Act in 1984 – the Young Offenders Act (YOA) – which replaced the Juvenile Delinquent Act (JDA) that was established back in 1908. JDA policies of operation had mixed child welfare needs with children's legal needs, and that was found to be unjust towards the youth, leading to unfair treatment. The YOA was designed to hold youth criminally responsible for their infractions through the courts and legal counsel while providing them with essential social, educational, psychological, and life-skills support. By addressing young people's developmental needs alongside their being held accountable for their violation of the law helped promote appropriate social behaviours that would ultimately afford them the best chance of becoming responsible, productive, and contributing adults in the future.

In 2003, the YOA was repealed and replaced with the Youth Criminal Justice Act (YCJA). It was felt that under the YOA, the courts were being excessively utilized to incarcerate young people with minor infractions, which could, instead, be dealt with in the community. This fit perfectly with my university course work, my fact-finding, interviewing skills, my report writing skills acquired through my Radio Arts diploma, and my passion for service. Being able to provide relief to others who were in need brought joy and added purpose to my existence.

In response to and in implementing the new laws dealing with young people involved with the criminal justice system, new youth correctional facilities were built and personnel were being solicited for these facilities throughout the province. The Strathmore Youth Development Centre (SYDC) was one of those provincial institutions. Strathmore is a small, farming town 50 kilometers east of Calgary. Due to its proximity to the City of Calgary, I was keenly interested in the opportunity. I felt it was time to leave Lethbridge, and therefore, I applied for the position and mailed in my application.

Within two weeks of submitting my application, I received a call inviting me for an interview. My stars were aligned and my confidence soared! Yet, on the other hand, I could not believe my luck.

I hurriedly informed my supervisor at my day job of this upcoming interview date. I then went on to explain that I required a day off without pay. To my amazement, she informed me that I was in fact entitled to a day off *with* pay since I was still interviewing with the same employer, the Government of Alberta. Needless to say, I was pleasantly surprised.

While I have met a few bad people throughout my journey in life, I must say that all the good, kind, and helpful people I have encountered along the way have compensated for any bad experiences with others. What followed that conversation with my supervisor was one of those great experiences of being on the receiving end of truly kind and generous people. My supervisor not only gave me the day off to attend the interview, she also supplied me with a work reference. Going the extra mile, she assisted me in preparing for the interview, putting me through a general knowledge, mock interview because that was the service we provided for our own clients at the office. Her generosity in providing such kind help and service to me in preparation for this interview was deeply appreciated.

On my own, I continued to prepare for the rest of the interview by digging through the specifics of the old Act, the provisions of the new Act, particularly its rehabilitative advantages for young people. In addition, Derin and I drove to Calgary early in the morning on the day of the interview and continued east to Strathmore to tour the facility before my assigned interview time in the afternoon. As a result, I was able to deliver interview answers that were relevant to the physical environment of the Centre.

For me, it has always been very important to over prepare for interviews rather than be not prepared enough. I like to give my all, for I've found it always pays off in the end. With regard to this new opportunity, I felt I could not afford to miss the prospect of gaining a full-time, permanent position that would help our family begin the next stage of our lives.

We finished the tour of SYDC. Then, we had lunch where I spent the extra time I had before my interview to review my notes. Being a planner, I didn't like being rushed for important meetings. Therefore, I arrived fifteen minutes early to the interview venue located in downtown Calgary. First impressions count, and I was determined to make a favourable impression.

A Human Resources representative, a manager, and a supervisor from SYDC interviewed me. I felt a real connection with the interview panel and was confident about my presentation. Two weeks later, I received the job offer.

The offer required that I act promptly in order to meet the training start date of August 10th, 1984. I was required to provide a telefax number to the office so that a complete package of the offer could be faxed to me. As part of the process, I needed to review the conditions of the offer, sign the forms, and return them to Human Resources.

I viewed the offer as being very good, but it was conditional to many prerequisites. First, I had to complete and pass a series of tests: physical-fitness, medical, criminal, and child welfare checks, plus written tests. I was on top of the world, but I was also under an enormous amount of pressure with all these upcoming tests. Good fortune sometimes brings pressure, you know.

The toughest part of my newfound success was the need to make quick but long-lasting decisions. It was already late June, and I had to first tender resignation letters for my current positions at SACLA and Social Services. Although I had settled in well with most of my colleagues and created a few special friendships, it was time to bid farewell. Next, we needed to give notice to our landlord and search for a new accommodation in Calgary. We were also leaving all our friends and many great relationships behind to start afresh in Calgary. I was excited but quietly scared. Due to the time sensitivity of all the notices I had to supply, I followed up vigorously with Human Resources regarding my new job to ascertain whether all my papers had been received and get my training start date confirmed in writing before I tendered any of my resignations or served any notices.

After I received the offer with a confirmed start date indicating that my employment was approved, everything else in Lethbridge was set in motion. There were many farewell luncheons and barbeques held for us by work colleagues, neighbours, and friends like Lynda, Gloria, and Mitch. We were finishing up one chapter in our lives and preparing for the start of a new one.

My husband and I along with the girls then set out on a weekend trip to Calgary to try and find accommodations starting the month of August. Because my new workplace was in the town of Strathmore east of Calgary, we focused our search on the eastern end of the city. Something incredible happened during our search, which alleviated some of my anxieties about home searches. With memories of the bad landlady experience from Lethbridge and previous negative experiences in Calgary, I was pleasantly surprised by how much the culture of tolerance within the city had evolved since being away from Calgary for almost six years.

In previous years, making an enquiry with a distinct accent on the phone about a vacant suite for rent would result in an "oh no, the place is already rented" reply. Then, after putting my non-immigrant friends on the phone minutes later to ask to come and view the same unit, the person on the other end would invite them to come see the unit that I had just been told was unavailable. I can't recall how many times I heard that dismissive phrase on the line. Thus, I pondered whether landlords had become more tolerant and accepting of other cultures, colours, and accents or if the economic climate of the time forced their tolerance of renting to minorities. Regardless of the meaning behind this shift, we were pleased to experience this new atmosphere of acceptance in our search for new accommodations.

We ended up having many vacancies to choose from that were available to us. After considering all the options, we settled on a two-bedroom apartment on the southeast edge of the city. The location was close to all the amenities we needed with easy access in and out of the city. We had a great weekend in Calgary scouting out and locating all the necessary services we would need including daycare, schools, shopping, banking, and employment possibilities for my husband.

After we returned to Lethbridge, the month of July was spent packing up, enjoying the summer, and saying goodbyes to our many friends and colleagues. In addition, I started to prepare my body for the pending, grueling, physical demands of my new job by exercising regularly, which was not especially difficult for me. I had been quite athletic throughout my elementary and high school years, participating in track and field events along with football (soccer) and table tennis (ping-pong). Therefore, getting back into a regular, physical routine was not too difficult. I also continued working at both SACLA and with Social Services until the end of July. My vacation days that year were the ten days between moving and the start of my new job in Strathmore.

We moved in on August 1st, 1984, which provided us a few days to set up and get settled in before I had to report for training on August 10th. We had contracted a small moving company to haul our big furniture items to Calgary for us. They arrived a day before we needed to be out of our Lethbridge apartment, and we set out on our way the following day. We packed up small items and supplies we would need to sustain us for the day plus a night at a hotel before we could take possession of our new apartment. Everything about our departure from Lethbridge went smoothly – the kids were well behaved and settled easily into the road trip while we reminisced about this last chapter of our lives and shared our hopes and plans for our immediate future.

Three quarters of the way into our journey, we suddenly noticed that our modest, blue, Suzuki jalopy began to slow down dramatically even with a completely depressed gas pedal. We parked and inspected the vehicle as much as we could, but nothing seemed to be out of the ordinary as far as we could see. Unfortunately, our mechanical knowledge was next to nothing, and we had no idea what to check for or look at. Still concerned, we bravely continued our drive.

The drive didn't get any better. It felt like we were only inching closer to our destination, for we had to make many stops along the way to give the vehicle a rest when it demanded one. It would stall...then, we would have to brake and restart it again. We would travel some distance, only to have to repeat the same cycle over and over until we finally reached the edge of the city limits on Macleod Trail. We could have continued to push towards our hotel, but the vehicle at that point had started to emit smoke, which we figured was a sign of a much bigger problem. So, we decided to call the Alberta Motor Association

(AMA) from the first pay phone we saw (there were still no cell phones back then) to get some roadside assistance.

Our leisurely trip from Lethbridge to Calgary that was supposed to take approximately five hours had now extended to more than eight hours of travel. The night was drawn, as it was about nine o'clock in the evening already. The babies were cranky, and we were tired. It had been an extremely long day already.

We called AMA, asking them to tow our vehicle to a mechanic's garage closer to the hotel where we were going to be staying for the night. We figured that, economically speaking, we could then get a ride with the tow truck driver, taking the few necessary items we would need from our vehicle for the night, and sort everything else out the following morning. Problem solved, right? Well, not so fast!

The AMA driver arrived. We explained to him what had happened and the services we required, including a ride along to the mechanic's shop from where we would walk to the hotel. The driver didn't respond either way but went back and climbed into his truck and took a long while to return. With the babies still inside the jeep, my husband and I remained by our vehicle waiting for the tow truck driver to return.

Just as he was getting out of his truck, *three* police cruisers arrived and surrounded us. We were shocked and petrified! Our prior experience with the police in Lethbridge had not been positive, and sadly, this one was not any better. In fact, it was far worse!

A total of five officers emerged from the three police cruisers. Two officers spoke to the driver before marching towards us while the remaining three officers stood sternly on guard. They did not ask us any questions. They merely proclaimed that the driver had been afraid for his life and had called them for protection. Completely flabbergasted, we attempted to explain our situation to them and the fact that we simply needed roadside assistance along with a ride to the mechanic's shop. The more we attempted to get any help from them, the more they became aggressive towards Derin. It appeared as if they were looking for any reason to manhandle him.

The road was dark with very little traffic. They ordered us to remove our kids from the vehicle and anything essential that we wanted from the jeep. Then, the tow truck driver hooked up the jeep and drove off. To our utmost dismay and extreme sadness, these five officers then got into their cruisers and took off without another word, leaving us stranded in the empty parking lot without any consideration for our entire family's safety. We didn't understand how they could come to the aid of a single, tow truck driver who said he was afraid of a young black couple with two young children, yet leave us there in the dark with no assistance. It was without question not the best end to what had started out to be a day of hope regarding the next chapter in our lives.

Along with our three-year-old and ten-month-old daughters, we trudged back to the phone booth my husband had used earlier and called for a taxi. Completely drained, we arrived at the hotel shortly before midnight, very shaken up by what we'd just experienced at the hands of the police. We settled our babies in for the night, but my husband and I had a restless night. Our sense of hope and enthusiasm for the future that had begun our trip to Calgary was now replaced with uncertainty.

The morning of August 1st, 1984, arrived sooner than anticipated. Checking out of the hotel, we set out to find out what was wrong with our vehicle and the cost of repair. It turned out that the carburetor had overheated, and we would have to leave our vehicle at the shop for the day.

In this encounter, however, we were met with much welcomed kindness. The mechanic's shop owner spared one of his workers and work vehicles to drive us along with our belongings to our new apartment. After the repairs were completed, he sent the same worker back to pick up my husband and bring him to the shop to get our jeep. We were so grateful for the kind and considerate care and service. Returning the blessing, we went on to use that shop for all our vehicle maintenance and repairs for as long as it was in business.

The unfair and intimidating treatment we received from both the officers and the tow truck driver that night was both horrible and unforgettable. Yet, a single person's humane gesture of kindness refuted our negative experience with a renewed belief in humanity. The experience also heightened my sense of justice and injustice.

We could have followed up with a complaint, and you may wonder why we didn't. However, in those days, one's rights were not readily publicized or respected, and there was a lack of access to services through which we could defend our rights. It would have been totally counterproductive to file a complaint with the members of the same organization who had mistreated us. It was unheard of and could have resulted in further mistreatment and end up being a huge waste of our precious time. In the end, we chose to go our own way but with a resolve, particularly within myself, to work towards fair and just treatment for all. As a result, I have dedicated myself to causes that provide voices for marginalized youth, that educate police recruits through my role as an advisory board member, and that assist new immigrants in the city.

Chapter 4

CAREER – INCEPTION

On August 10th, 1984, I arrived at the Strathmore Youth Development Centre (SYDC) to begin my six-week-long, training program as a youth worker, officially titled Correctional Services Worker (CSW 1-2). My preliminary, job offer letter depended on me passing all my classes, including physical fitness. The main courses I had to take were: Report Writing – for the courts and for case management; Effective Interviewing Techniques; Behaviour Management; Understanding and Interpretation of the Young Offenders Act in reference to the Canadian Criminal Code; Security Awareness (including physical and facility searches); Contraband Identification, Handling, and Preservation of Evidence; Program Delivery; First Aid and CPR.

We started classes early, and the training was very rigorous, making each day go by quickly. The mornings were spent in the classroom. Then, the first half of the afternoon was spent alternating between practicing either First Aid/CPR or conducting searches. During searches, the trainers planted contraband items on volunteers for the body search and in a living unit for the unit search. Then, we were graded on our individual, recovery success. The later part of each afternoon was always reserved for physical training out in the field or jogging through the town of Strathmore.

I enjoyed my training and learning very much for the most part...except towards the end of each day. I have always been fascinated by new discoveries, and acquiring new knowledge has always thrilled me, but by the end of the afternoon, I was miserable. Are you confused yet? Well, don't be. Let me explain...

At the end of the day after the physical training part had ended, I would find myself sneezing uncontrollably. My eyes would swell up, and my nose would get congested. I would be dripping nonstop from both eyes and nose, leaving me feeling quite uncomfortable. Afterwards, I couldn't comprehend much of anything that was taught after we returned to the classroom in the late afternoon to wrap things up. For the remainder of the evening at home, I continued to be miserable. The next morning, however, I would be feeling all right and more than ready for the start of another training day.

This cycle went on and on with me persevering and pushing to get through that first week. The Friday of my first week of training finally arrived. Upon my return home looking like Rudolph the Red-Nosed Reindeer along with swollen eyes and a scratchy voice, my husband insisted I go to a walk-in, medical clinic to find out what was wrong. Upon seeing the doctor, I was told that I was allergic to hay and pollen. Now, it finally

94

made sense to me that, if I was going to enjoy the outdoors, especially on a windy day in the western prairies of Canada, I must first ingest an antihistamine to combat my allergy symptoms. Reactine and the like became my regular companion for the duration of my outdoor training sessions and beyond. I was very thankful that I would finally be able to enjoy *all* my learning without feeling miserable.

I was in the training program with fifteen other candidates from diverse academic backgrounds. However, none of them looked like me, sounded like me, nor did any have young toddlers or babies to care for at home like me. Again, I stood out as different in more than one way.

Although the class was small like my college days, it was void of the intimacy and camaraderie I enjoyed in the Radio Arts program. Instead, it reminded me of university experiences where, as an immigrant, I constantly had to prove that I belonged. Back then, most Canadian students ignored my existence and avoided contact. Then, there were others who were curious, and in their lack of awareness, asked me unflattering questions about my birth continent – Africa – when they meant to ask about my birth country – Nigeria. It did end up being an opportunity for me to educate those who asked though. Eventually, most of my fellow students came around and accepted me when they realized that I could hold my own both academically and intellectually.

Being in this training program was not much different. Once again, I had to prove myself. I had to prove that, not only did I belong, but my skills were equal if not superior to my classmates.

As a child, I was told that I had what it took to be successful at anything I chose to do. Therefore, I have always been driven to achieve and have never been afraid to venture out in order to accomplish things and be a success. As a result, it was not a coincidence that, being an immigrant, I learnt to over prepare, over educate, and over extend myself to stand apart from the rest of the pack. It was an instinct to work harder to not afford any of the trainers an excuse to deem me unqualified or unsuitable for the position. Consequently, I gave my all in training, more than willing to prove myself capable and qualified.

While most of my classmates stuck to their own group, I did meet two young women that I could relate to, Eileen Kwan and Lonnie Melvyn. Eileen was a young lady of Asian descent whose parents were immigrants from Hong Kong. She had been brought to Canada as a young child, and therefore, she did not have an accent like me. However, with this background and understanding, Eileen Kwan was drawn to me, and we instantly became friends.

Eileen became instrumental in my professional world in those early days in many ways. For example, when I would join others at a dining table only to have them quietly leave the table or the room altogether, she was not afraid to stay and spend time with me. We ended up spending our break times together, which I really appreciated.

Lonnie Melvyn relocated to Calgary from Edmonton for this training and employment. We also connected as friends. Both she and Eileen became carpool partners with me over the course of four years of driving back and forth between Strathmore and Calgary.

Although it was tough to face the challenges of suspicion, rejection, and discrimination due to my status as an immigrant with all my "differences", I have found that finding a few giving and accepting people can make all the difference in the world. Connecting with Eileen and Lonnie became the difference during my time at SYDC.

With regard to class content, there were some interesting and challenging techniques taught in order to serve the youth we would be dealing with in the best possible way. My previous training in interviewing and report writing from Radio Arts proved beneficial in the recruit training classes. However, writing and interviewing techniques for the courts and the justice system was very different. It involved court reporting that was more factual in nature with a clear summary of the reporter's opinions at the end. Interviewing skills needed to take on a more interrogative style yet be equally non-threatening in order to extract the information needed for the benefit of the youth's future. Then, there were motivational interviewing techniques that were used for developing specialized case plans for each adolescent. These methods were primarily used to gather a complete history on each young person to facilitate the development of a comprehensive, rehabilitative plan. The interview, along with the ultimate plan that was developed as a result, involved the youth, a parent or legal guardian, the youth's school, and other stakeholders. I was also exposed to cause and effect, behavior management techniques as well as educative, life skills development programming that were highly beneficial once I began my duties as a youth worker. I totally immersed myself in my training in order to be ready to be the best I could be as a Correctional Services Worker for the young people I would be serving.

An intense six weeks of training was finally completed. My hard work paid off, and I passed all my classes, passed the child welfare check as well as the criminal record clearance, and my educational certificates were verified and validated. I was officially given the position I had worked so hard for!

Included in my official, job offer letter was information on the benefits package, the union to which I would belong, and my salary offer. What I was offered appeared to be totally reasonable since I had never made that much before, nor had I had a benefits package since working for the hospital prior to pursuing my higher education. Therefore, I eagerly signed my commencement papers and returned them to the personnel office before they could change their minds about their offer.

Approximately six months later, I discovered that I had been seriously shortchanged. Eileen and I were driving home from work one day, and our conversation veered to her plans to return to school to obtain her degree since she only had a college diploma at the time. This discussion ultimately extended to our employment, our qualifications, and the government's salary scales. We discovered that we had both been placed on the same salary scale despite the fact that I possess both a college diploma *and* a university degree.

The importance of this discrepancy was initially lost on me. I was just happy to be able to apply my education to the career that I was building in serving others. Plus, as an immigrant, I felt like I was one of the lucky ones. Hence, I was reluctant at the time to rock the boat by complaining.

With persistence and encouragement from Eileen, however, I summed up enough courage to discuss the discrepancy with my first unit supervisor, who also happened to have been one of the panel members from my initial interview. His name was Chester Uszacki, and he was a very good supervisor. He supervised through teaching, coaching, and being genuinely supportive of both the youth and staff.

Chester came to Canada as a child with his parents who emigrated from Poland. I suspect that, because of his own struggles as a young immigrant who experienced difficulties with the English language, he was especially kind towards me. Thus, he was generous with his time, showing me the ropes for how to succeed on the job. I especially remember a statement he made to me during one of our coaching sessions together that really bolstered my confidence. He stated that my demonstrated confidence and tenacity at my interview compensated for any lack of direct experience for the job, and he was certain that I was going to do well. Needless to say, Chester became one of my mentors.

So, after being well equipped with a dose of confidence from Eileen and a copy of her pay stub as proof, I shared the discrepancy with Chester, who immediately pulled out a copy of the Provincial Employees Bargaining Unit Agreement to consult with. We did, in fact, establish that I was definitely being underpaid. He then proceeded to outline the steps I needed to take, including his providing me with contact names at the personnel office so that I could confront the powers that be of the discrepancy.

Thinking that this was an honest mistake, I followed up, fully expecting that it would be swiftly corrected once I submitted all the proof and supporting documentation. Boy, was I naïve to the core! What should've been an easy fix based on qualifications and policy ended up being a lesson in perseverance in going after what I was rightfully entitled to. I learnt that you sometimes have to push for what is rightfully and justly yours.

First, I spoke to the person who signed my employment offer letter, but he insisted that I was being paid according to my qualifications. I then reminded him of what my credentials were and offered to resubmit my certificates, all to no avail. Next, I consulted with Chester again, who insisted that I was being cheated and supplied me with the name of the manager in charge of Human Resources. It took several telephone calls and messages before hearing back from a lady by the name of Donna MacDonald. Donna reassured me that she would look into the matter and get back to me. Within one week, I received a letter from her stating that there was indeed a mistake made with regard to my pay scale, and it would be rectified by the next pay period. The letter also indicated that I would receive back pay for the six months that I had already worked under the wrong salary amount.

Eileen, Chester, and Donna all advocated for me, directly or indirectly. This demonstrated to me that there really were good, fair-minded people all around me. Where it had initially appeared that I was alone on an island in this new workplace, the kindness of others reached out and blessed me. I will be forever thankful to them for their part in helping me get to where I am today.

My new workplace was structured and run quite differently compared to your typical office and schedule. It consisted of four, separate cottages divided into two sides or units per cottage. This meant that there were eight units in total. Each cottage was assigned two youth workers who worked on rotational day and afternoon shifts on a 'six days on, three days off' schedule. Staffing consisted of a unit supervisor, a team leader, and a team manager supported by the programs department, recreation staff, the school, the house parents, and administration. Administration included the Director of the Centre, the Assistant Director, the Business Manager, and support staff. There was also a psychologist, a contract psychiatrist, and a chaplain assigned to the Centre and involved in the work. The Centre was a twenty-four hour operation with three shifts: 6:45 a.m. to 3:00 p.m., 2:45 p.m. to 11:00 p.m., and 10:45 p.m. to 7:00 a.m. Being as I and the other youth workers worked only day or afternoon shifts, there were correctional officers who covered the night shifts.

There were three rotational teams, and I was assigned to "C" Team. My first unit partner was a wonderful lady named Barbara (Barb) McKnight who became one of my closest sister friends since the first day we met. Barb was part of the first group of recruits, and she had started on the job approximately two months prior to me coming on staff. She had been part of a wave of young people who moved west from Ontario in search

102

of employment opportunities in the mid-1980s. Barb had worked with troubled youth in group homes before, both in Ontario and Calgary, and possessed an enormous amount of skill and insight into dealing with teenagers. She was endlessly patient and caring and came up with many programming ideas that were of great benefit to me in my work.

Barb and I bonded almost immediately. We shared our life stories and discovered that we had some common background, similar work ethic, and parallel aspirations. She was a great teacher and partner early in my career and a life-long supporter throughout my career as a civil servant. As a matter of fact, both our careers have mirrored each other to the extent that we commenced within months of each other in the same institution and retired within months of each other in another but same institution. We became family friends, sharing many memorable moments together including that of raising our children. I am as happy for Barb as she is of her retirement to a cottage in Ontario and to the sunny and hot Yuma, Arizona, during the winter months. We both have worked tirelessly for the betterment of the lives we have worked with, and we've given our best in the way of support for each other in all areas.

Working with co-ed teenagers aged twelve to eighteen who had broken the law was very challenging and exhilarating at the same time. I encountered the natural mood swings associated with surging hormones and testosterone, all the way to parental

103

neglect, abandonment issues, maladjustments, special needs, and substance abuse problems just to mention a few. There was a lot to learn in a very short time, but I was determined to make a difference in the lives of the young people I was put in charge of.

Most of the youth in SYDC had experienced various degrees of trauma of all types in their short lives and had grown to mistrust adults, resulting in them having little to no regard for authority. I began to apply the behavior management techniques I learnt in training in combination with theories from my crime and delinquency courses. It was during this time that I truly realized the importance of positively engaging these troubled young people in order to build trust with them. In doing so, I could then get to the core of their challenges, assist them in the healing process by providing the resources and tools necessary to deal with those challenges, and help them to become productive individuals moving forward.

For teenagers, any idle time is a wasted opportunity for self-discovery. At SYDC, we provided stability, normalcy, and age appropriate, developmental opportunities in their lives through various programming, including recreation, homework period, cooking, baking, art, storytelling, board games, personal care and self-esteem building, group work, and basic living skills classes. Above all, we taught them self-discipline and how to abide by the law. As challenging as some of these youth and their circumstances were, this was the beginning of a very rewarding time in my life and career.

Here is an excerpt from Donna[3], one of the special young people I was privileged to work with:

"I know for me, I've never forgotten you and your kindness and compassion. I'm sure there are so many more kids that have been influenced by you as well. We need more like you in this world, especially in the way of troubled kids. I remember vividly like it was yesterday the things you did to make me feel safe and that "I mattered", things I never had before."

SYDC was an "open custody" institution, which meant that while the adolescents were legally held under warrants, the facility had no locks. It was a twenty-four hour operation with unlocked doors and windows with only a perimeter fence to keep the public out. As such, the residents had opportunities to escape, and they did so from time to time with staff in hot pursuit. Despite the risks, the principle behind the unlocked doors was to encourage the development of law-abiding, natural compliance behaviours. In addition, the many types of

---

[3] Name changed to protect identity

programs we ran with the youth also reflected the encouragement to become law-abiding citizens.

There were many positive and not so positive moments throughout the years I spent at the Centre. When dealing with troubled young people, you are bound to experience many ups and downs, exhilarating breakthroughs and discouraging setbacks. There were a few moments of crises that we encountered that stand out in my memory. They highlight the challenges we faced in trying to help reform the youth in our care.

On one particular shift, I decided that Barb and I would run a hide-and-seek program with the residents. Everything was going rather well. The kids were having fun and so were we. Then, we announced that the third round of the game would be the last round before dinner. Well, I guess one certain young person did not want the game to end…and decided to go into hiding permanently. He ran away!

Accounting for all residents under my care and supervision at all times was, by far, one of the most crucial responsibilities of my entire career. There are a few mishaps that people who work in custodial institutions dread the most, and one of them is the loss of a client/resident/young person. Losing track of one under your charge brings an enormous amount of attention and stress onto the entire facility and the staff on duty.

Our fun-filled shift came to an abrupt halt with the Centre shutting down to look for the escapee. All movement ceased, and every nook, cranny, and crevice of the Centre, plus its surroundings, was searched to no avail. The police were called and a description of the teenager provided. The shift manager notified the Centre Director who, in turn, notified the Executive Director in Edmonton, and many reports were generated.

Our fun and easy shift turned out to be a long and stressful one. There was no more hide-and-seek played for a long time afterwards as a result of this unfortunate end to what had started out to be an enjoyable day for all. Furthermore, the escapee felt the wrath of his peers for spoiling the game after he was recaptured and returned to the Centre with a new charge of escaping lawful custody.

We also went on field trips in an effort to normalize the kids' lives and promote healthy development. On one of those trips, we took a group to Carseland Provincial Park for an afternoon picnic. Unfortunately, one of them, a particularly young but system-wise boy, broke into an unoccupied, vacation cabin and stole a hunting rifle. We wouldn't have noticed anything was amiss if it hadn't been for one of the other boys who "ratted" him out. We had to report the incident to the police who filed charges of break and enter and theft against the boy. Many more interviews ensued with the other youth, followed by numerous staff reports and a group session to review the incident.

When the Village Square Leisure Centre in northeast Calgary newly opened, we took a mixed group of girls and boys on an outing for swimming. One of the girls requested to go to the bathroom. Unbeknownst to us, she had scoped out a nearby drug store earlier, and on her "bathroom" break, went in and stole a pack of Gravol. By the time we finished swimming and were heading back to the Centre, the effects of the drug had begun to take a toll on the girl, for she had taken more than the standard dose. Naturally, we all went into panic mode, for we knew not what was causing her symptoms. As was often the case, through the rapport and trust we had built with some of the youth, someone was willing to come forward and tell us what the girl had ingested. We immediately sought medical assistance for the young lady and suspended her from future leisure outings.

These incidences show just how challenging it could be to help these kids get to the place of making better decisions. Much was dependent on establishing healthier mentalities and emotional stability within each individual. We worked hard to provide a balance of activities and programs alongside the rules and boundaries. We wanted the youth to feel like they were normal, yet we had to be ever cognizant of why they were there in the first place and the things they still needed to work through.   As you can see, this led to the occasional crisis or setback.   However, knowing what these kids came from and where they started, it also meant that the victories were that much sweeter once achieved, no matter how small those victories were.

Barb and I were together for approximately one year when she went on maternity leave after giving birth to her son Trent, who is now a young civil engineer with the federal government out in Saskatchewan.   During her absence, I worked with a few different partners who exhibited less than ideal work ethics. This made me value Barb's partnership even more.   Upon her return, we continued our important work together with these troubled young people while at the same time pondering our own futures and what they had in store.

Barb soon applied for a supervisory position.   We both entertained high hopes that she would get the job.   She did, of course, for her drive, excellence of service, and superior work ethic made her an excellent candidate for the job.   The only downside was that we were soon separated as partners. Although we were no longer together on the unit, we were still on the same team, which allowed us to continue to carpool.   We also would spend time together on days off from time to time.

Among the different partners I worked with after Barb was promoted was a fellow named Ken[4]. Ken had been transferred to SYDC from one of the adult institutions and placed with me without much introduction. He just appeared one day, and I was informed that Ken was my new unit partner. Being six months pregnant with my son at the time and knowing that I would soon be leaving on maternity leave, I didn't complain too much about the frequent staff changes and the instability it caused on the unit, especially for the young people.

However, it wasn't too long before pleasant, polite, somewhat timid Ken became problematic. I had boys and girls on both sides of the unit needing specialized attention and care...and now I had a grown man to take care of! Sadly, it turned out that Ken was an alcoholic who drank from his coke bottle throughout the shift and hid in the office reading newspapers while I took care of the kids' needs. As a result, I was saddled with the fallout resulting from Ken's issues, and in my pregnant condition no less, for as my partner on the unit, his performance and habits negatively impacted everybody.

Of course, something had to give, and it finally did. Unit cleanliness and upkeep were not up to standard to the point of intervention by Susan Lewerkcy, the Centre's Director at the time. On this particular day, Susan ordered that neither Ken nor

---

[4] Name changed to protect identity

I could go home until we had supervised and assisted the youth in cleaning the unit from top to bottom properly. My 6:45 a.m. to 3:00 p.m. shift ended at 8:00 p.m. that day...and I was due to report for duty again the following morning at 6:45 a.m. Exhausted but dedicated nonetheless, I reported for work the next day despite my fatigue. Ken, however, booked off 'sick'. Once again, I had to work my shift with yet another, different and unfamiliar person.

After this incident, I summoned up the courage to approach the Director with my concerns because it looked like nobody was prepared to look after my welfare at that point except me. Specifically, I shared my medical concerns with her in how I was being overly relied upon to carry out two people's responsibilities on the unit due to Ken's performance. Amazingly, she understood my concerns and offered me a choice I couldn't refuse. The first option would allow me to stay on my unit, and they would move Ken. The drawback to this choice was that I would have to work with two different people sharing the position as my partner. Option number two was that I could temporarily cover a Community Liaison Coordinator position looking after school placements, job searches and placements, resume building, along with counselling and coaching until I left for my maternity leave. The best choice was a no brainer for me. I love changes and meaningful challenges. I thrive on value-added opportunities and contributing to people's lives, especially young people's lives! I chose to take on the position as Community Liaison Coordinator and held this position until my son was born in August 1986.

Our son was named Adedeji (Deji), meaning "double crown". Deji arrived exactly on his anticipated due date of August 6th, 1986, weighing in at 7 pounds 14 ounces (3.572 kilograms). His delivery was equally precise, making his appearance within one hour of arriving at the hospital. This was a sign of what was to come, for he is still punctual today.

My husband was very happy to welcome a son into the family. The girls were ecstatic to have a baby brother, and they both doted on him. Our family was complete.

For the first time, I enjoyed a maternity leave of six months, and it was very much appreciated. I was able to give my undivided focus to my children, my husband, and my home. One surprising activity that the girls and I did a lot of was baking and cooking. I had gone from not liking cooking at all in those early days of being a new immigrant when some well-meaning sister friends had encouraged me to embark on a cooking career to now being able to embrace this domestic skill with my family. I had actually learnt to appreciate cooking from the house parents at SYDC. They cooked during the week and left menus for us to prepare on the weekends with the residents. This allowed me to ease into food preparation and to experiment with baking. Getting bolder in my newfound skill, I acquired recipes and learnt to prepare many western dishes. So, the girls and I enjoyed our times in the kitchen. We also swam, biked, and visited the library. I had always volunteered at Lolade's (Loly's) school whenever possible, and this break from work allowed me to do more of that. I really appreciated this time off with my family.

February 1987 arrived too soon, and I had to return to work. It was hard to leave my son with a babysitter for the first time, and my daughters had gotten accustomed to me being at home twenty-four seven. Finding a reputable childcare provider for all the children was my new challenge.

Between my shift work and my husband's schedule, we only required part-time, often evening care. We also didn't want our infant son going to daycare so early. Therefore, we decided on hiring a nanny who would come into our home as needed. This would also allow Lolade to be able to walk home after school. The arrangement was effective until I found out that the one nanny spent all her time on my telephone, tying up the line (no call waiting feature or mobile phones back then). This made it difficult to get through and check on the children while on one of my breaks. The second nanny was great with my children but did her grocery shopping from my fridge and freezer. Eventually, we found Barb and Tim Bagby who lived and ran a dayhome in our neighbourhood behind the elementary school my daughters attended. They were wonderful people! Lolade collected

Adejoke after school and they both walked over to Barb's house where I'd dropped off Deji on my way to my afternoon shift. Then, my husband picked them up after he finished work. They were extremely flexible with our work schedules, and the children remained with them for many years until we moved away from the neighbourhood.

I returned to my unit position to another female partner. Coincidentally, my new partner and I had attended the same university together and had run into each other a few times prior to working at SYDC. She was friendly, articulate, and could relate to the young people well, but that was it unfortunately. Any other job-related responsibilities were not a priority to her. Unit cleanliness, case management, caseload notes, filing, and so on were neglected. Once again, I found myself compensating for my partner's lack of productivity. At least she wasn't a drunk, so I tolerated her weaknesses and persevered.

Then, an acting supervisor opportunity for my unit became available, and I applied. Shockingly, I was passed over, and my new partner was given the position instead. Again, I felt compelled to stand up for myself in light of this blatant oversight. I approached my shift manager and queried as to how he and his decision-making team members found my partner to be more capable of managing all the staff, the residents, and other responsibilities associated with that position as opposed to me, and why my contributions along with my dedication to *all* my duties were overlooked and not considered. His response infuriated me...and he didn't understand why. He told me that the kids needed someone strong and who was respected – like me – on the floor. He thought he was paying me a compliment! Of course, I retorted by asking him if he thought marginalizing a capable, competent, committed employee while promoting someone who was inept was fair. Not surprisingly, he had no answer to my valid question.

This action was another piece of evidence of a workplace clique, one that I was not a part of and did not plan to be a part of. I was not created to fit into a clique. I was my own unique person who relied on my own skills and capabilities. I did not need a group to define who I was or what I was entitled to. With this resolution in mind, I continued in my unit position with an even stronger determination to advance my career despite the possible obstacles ahead, including unfair practices and discrimination.

Thankfully, another acting supervisory opportunity became available. This time, my application was successful. I assumed Unit Supervisor responsibilities part of the time and Team Lead responsibilities at other times.

Later on, a satellite group home, North Haven, was opened in 1988 to serve residents transitioning back into the community from SYDC and the Calgary Young Offender Centre (CYOC). I applied to join the team being formed to operate this new, community facility and was accepted. Once again, I was excited to take on this new challenge and the opportunity to invest in the lives of young people.

Shortly before the opening of the North Haven Group Home, a young lady was transferred from the Edmonton Young Offender Centre (EYOC) to Strathmore as a Team Leader. Her name was Ramona Deer. Ramona and I were immediately drawn to each other for a reason that was not evident until we both got to the group home.

Ramona was hired as Manager of North Haven, and I left SYDC to become the acting Assistant Manager. As we worked together, we began to share our individual and family histories, and in the process, grew closer as friends. Ramona's parents were immigrants like me. Her mother emigrated from Germany after the Second World War, and her father had been a railway labourer from China and had passed away when she was ten years old. Although Ramona was born in Edmonton, Alberta, through the stories and experiences of her parents, she could relate to some of the challenges faced by me and many other immigrants. Our connection grew deeper, and we have been sister friends ever since.

At North Haven, we received youth on temporary absence passes from CYOC, SYDC, and sometimes EYOC. Temporary absence passes allowed these kids to access community programming such as schooling, additional training, specialized treatments, and employment. We collaborated with all stakeholders including parents/guardians, the police, probation officers, prospective employers, schools, and treatment providers to develop concrete, workable plans for each individual. Our purpose was to facilitate their successful reintegration into the community and in ultimately becoming productive citizens.

We also facilitated parenting group sessions. It was extremely important to promote effective communication between each teenager and their parent(s). These sessions worked with each party to improve their communication and work through the difficulties of the past.

Being able to develop concrete, results-based, case plans for the youth at North Haven was very fulfilling. Observing each young person work hard on their plans, achieve their set goals, and move on to better their lives fueled my passion for service and for helping people, especially young people.

Unfortunately, approximately twelve months later in the first quarter of 1989, the group home program was contracted out to a local, community, youth agency. Since this meant the current staff would be replaced, we were offered a chance to return to SYDC. For me, I viewed this development as an opportunity to move forward to another centre instead of returning to SYDC.

Up until this point, I had had no working experience in a secure, maximum-security, youth facility. Yet, that did not deter me from putting in a request to move on to the Calgary Young Offender Centre. Rather than being afraid of future uncertainties and challenges, the excitement of the unknown truly intrigued and motivated me. My request was approved, and I chose to take a few days off to reflect on my journey thus far and to prepare myself for this new adventure.

I had always followed my instincts, and my intuition to move on and continue my career development at CYOC rather than at SYDC was not any different. I was very thankful I followed that leading in the months that followed. In response to the economic climate of the time and the provincial government's fiscal restructuring, SYDC was gradually reduced to a shell of its glory days when I first started at the Centre. Ultimately, SYDC closed permanently in 1992, and many of the staff did not have a choice as to where they were next placed. I, on the other hand, had gotten to choose my placement when I left three years prior to its shutdown!

On April 1, 1989, I reported for duty at the Calgary Young Offender Centre for the first of six afternoon shifts. Stepping into this huge, highly secured, youth institution, I was put on the afternoon rotation with many other staff members. There was one, notable observation with regard to the staff on duty...I was the only black person in the lineup that day. This continued to be the case for many years afterwards as well.

Starting this new job, it became apparent that almost all the staff in the building had heard of me. Many had already formed opinions about me without having met me. Some of the opinions were favourable, while others were not. Those with a negative opinion held it, not because they knew me in person, but because, in their viewpoint, I "didn't belong" there. Some of these opinions even played a part in my unit assignment and in whom my unit partner was going to be. In their minds, I was to be tested, and they set me up accordingly. What they didn't consider was that this was not at all unexpected on my part. Although I had met and expected to meet kind and open-minded people in my daily life encounters, I had also learnt not to let my guard down when stepping into new territory. I was not afraid of anyone else's opinion, for I was prepared to be the best at what I was assigned to do in spite of the challenges thrown at me.

The first day on my new job at CYOC, I was assigned a housing unit occupied by twenty-three, female offenders ranging in ages from 12 to 18 years old and partnered with a newly-hired, casual staff member with no security experience. We were both thrown into extremely, unfamiliar and tough territory. Although I had acquired security skills from working at SYDC, I did not possess the level of knowledge and skill expected for a maximum-security facility. I was not provided any orientation, nor was I given a chance to familiarize myself with the unit or Centre's routines, but instead, had to learn the routines on the fly. Furthermore, I was not given the opportunity to review each offender's files to acquaint myself with what I would be dealing with. Survival mode kicked in, and I quietly told myself that I would not be defeated. This attitude has sustained me throughout my journey so far.

One of the offenders we had on the unit and specifically assigned to my caseload was a young lady designated in 1994 by the Alberta Court of Queen's Bench as a "Dangerous Offender". This designation was (and is) reserved for extremely violent offenders, which meant she could be incarcerated indefinitely. She was only the second female in Canada with such a designation at the time.

My new unit partner, was a very kind, gentle, and experienced youth worker from the community. Finding our first assignment daunting, she was petrified of the circumstances we were under and expected to deal with and did nothing to hide it from me. I shared my concerns and apprehensions with her as well. Mustering our courage, we both pledged to be a team and work the challenges together. We were determined to survive the next eight hours ahead of us.

Within thirty minutes of our arrival on our assigned unit, we called a unit meeting with all twenty-three girls to introduce ourselves, get to know them, and to outline our shift's schedule. Within minutes of the meeting starting, it was apparent who was in control of the unit. This dangerous offender intimidated the other girls and attempted to do the same with us. She boasted freely about how she had "run off" other staff members and how she "controlled" the unit. My earlier suspicion of being set up was confirmed. With no preparation or orientation, we had been given the toughest unit to manage. It was sink or swim!

My unit partner was already petrified, and the shift was going to be a long one if I didn't take charge of this girl and the situation straight away. She and I worked through that six-day rotation and survived...but she never returned to that unit again. It was a brutal week!

The unit assignment that was initially meant or viewed by me as a test or a set up for failure turned out to be a very positive and stimulating placement for me. Most of the female offenders I worked with were victims of their own crimes, with the majority of them having been involved in petty theft and prostitution. They stole to sustain themselves, and they prostituted themselves because they had been taken advantage of by adults in their lives who had beat them, put them on the street, and kept the money. Their lives were swirling in a cycle of self-destruction fueled by abuse, low self-worth, and substance abuse. My passion for helping young people, now exclusively girls, grew stronger and stronger. Made for this job, I rose to the challenge!

I developed and facilitated many life skills workshop groups with topics addressing the many issues faced by these girls. In addition, I established relationships with outside community agencies working with youth, many who came to the Centre to provide services and to work with the young people in preparation for their release into the community. One of those agencies was the Servants Anonymous Society (SAS) of Calgary, a nonprofit, women's organization that, to this day, provides aid to young women exiting the sex trade, gives support to those at risk of sexual exploitation, and helps them achieve sobriety. As a general rule, in order for a girl to be accepted into the SAS program, she was required to have a supportive sponsor.

One particular girl registered in the program was on the brink of being lost to the street permanently. She had become pregnant by her pimp-boyfriend and disowned by her parents. Against stated protocol, which prohibited any kind of association with the youth outside of the institution, I sponsored this young, bright girl. Although she had somehow been accepted into the SAS program, she lacked the much needed, adult support to be successful once released from custody. Under my sponsorship, this young lady, Klaris[5],

---

[5] Name changed to protect identity

delivered her baby, stayed in the SAS program until she was confident enough to leave the city to pursue her education, and did very well thereafter. I saw the need and the potential in this young teenager and instinctively knew I needed to go the extra mile to support her turnaround in life.

My mission in life is to contribute positively to humankind. I can't state it enough how my passion is for young people – our future. I get a deep, euphoric kind of feeling and a sense of extreme satisfaction when people are enabled to achieve their individual or collective goals and I have played a part, however small, in making them happen. Reconnecting with Klaris years later over a cup of coffee, now a mother of a teenaged daughter and a successful professional in her own right, was extremely gratifying. It was another reminder of why I do what I do and the reason and motivation behind my passion.

A provision under the Young Offenders Act was created called "Alternative Measures", a special program meant to address the incarceration rate of young offenders with minor, non-violent offences. It permitted cases to be dealt with in the community by allowing kids charged for the first time and with minor crimes to "accept responsibility" in a variety of ways for the alleged offence. Each teen had to be willing to participate in the program.

The advent of this new program gave me an opportunity to put my project management, communication, and interpersonal skills, along with my ability to relate with teenagers, into practice. I applied for and was successful at becoming the first Alternative Measures Program Coordinator for my Ministry – Alberta Solicitor General, Young Offender Branch – in the City of Calgary.

As Alternative Measures Coordinator from 1990 to 1994, I first operated out of the Community Probation Office inside Fording Place on 9th Avenue by Centre Street and later out of the old Court Annex building before it was demolished to make way for the current Calgary Courts Centre. The reason for meeting clients outside of the Calgary Young Offender Centre was because the Act's intention was to avoid unnecessary exposure of adolescents to a maximum-security institution. Therefore, I met each young person and their guardian(s) three times a week, including evenings, to accommodate the kids' schooling and the guardians' work schedules. I also benefitted from this new schedule. I worked Monday to Friday for longer hours, which allowed me to spend more weekends and statutory holidays with my family and friends.

Police agencies in the province, as well as the crown prosecutors' offices and defense lawyers' offices referred youth with minor law infractions such as shoplifting, vandalism, mischief, or transit payment violations to me for a suitability review. Referrals and the transfer of referrals came in from all over the country as well. Once I reviewed each referral, I would decide whether or not a meeting with the young offender in person was warranted or if just a warning letter was required. If it was necessary to meet in person to process the infraction(s), I sent a letter to the young person and to their parents/legal guardians outlining my contact information, the alleged infraction(s), and a meeting date and place. From there, I would work with each young person in conjunction with all other involved parties to reach a desirable conclusion that would facilitate each kid being able to move forward constructively, and hopefully, prevent further incidents down the road.

This position was very satisfying for me! I met many concerned, caring parents from all walks of life who shared a common wish for their children – they wanted them to be happy, well adjusted, and successful kids. I was more than happy to support them in that endeavour, providing the necessary guidance and resources to aid in that regard.

The Alternative Measures Program was a very effective provision under the law that promoted immediacy, accountability, and relevance within each situation. Each young person was contacted within a few weeks of the date that they encountered law enforcement agencies. From the youth's point of view, the circumstance(s) of their offence was reviewed and the reasoning and 'logic' behind the decisions they had made which brought them to me. This was processed in the presence of their guardians. Based on the gravity of their charges, consequences were assigned along with completion dates. Of course, consequences definitely had to fit the crimes in order for them to be impactful on the young people. These consequences ranged from a simple letter of apology to the victim or an essay on the costs and benefits of their poor decision, all the way to community service hours and monetary compensation. Each adolescent was given a deadline for his or her assignment(s) to be completed or submitted, with opportunities for an extension only when and if required. Failure to complete the program within a reasonable time resulted in a return to the crown prosecutor's office for prosecution, at which time a warrant would be issued for the youth's arrest, and most often, the case did not return to the Alternate Measures Program for further consideration. I personally met with hundreds of young people and their parents/guardians over the four years of running the program.

This position gave me one of the most gratifying highlights of my career. Approximately 90% of the kids completed the program successfully, and thus, we did not see many of them end up at the institution. Additionally, it was very rewarding to get letters and thank you notes from both the young people and their parents/guardians. Often, months and even years later, a young person would approach me in public at places like a shopping mall or a convenience store to introduce him or herself as one of the kids I had seen through the program. I even met one at a high-end, car dealership where he worked with pride. Even though I wouldn't recognize them when they came up to me, they had remembered the care they received, the chance to turn their lives around...and they were grateful. I must say that these meetings gave my life such fulfillment as I had the privilege to know that I had effected positive changes in their young lives and that they had made a lasting impact.

There is one memorable encounter I'd love to share. One day, I was at a mall, and a young, handsome man approached and greeted me politely. He told me that he and his parents met with me in the Alternative Measures Program. He reminded me of the case where he and his friends had gone on a rampage, vandalizing their community centre. He told me that the hardest thing that I got him to do was to face the community centre's administrator and apologize in person as well as perform community service hours for them in the way of compensation. Yet, the most valuable lesson he learnt was finding out just how much it cost the centre to operate, especially in volunteer manpower. That realization sobered him. Not only had he recognized me during our chance meeting in the mall, he had also seen me a few times at his junior high school after he had completed the program because he had been a classmate of my oldest daughter. He cheerfully told me that he was now an engineer and doing well. I was absolutely thrilled and wore a permanent grin on my face for the remainder of that day!

In late 1994, my term as the Alternative Measures Program Coordinator came to an end, and I returned to the floor as a youth worker at CYOC. I resumed my work with the female population initially. However, as necessity demanded, a program restructuring was initiated resulting in younger male offenders being moved into the same unit due to the decline in the female numbers being admitted into the institution. Thus, I ended up working with two different populations – boys aged 12 years to 14 years and girls aged 14 years to 18 years, all with different needs and temperaments. Imagine twelve pubescent boys with their age expected immaturity housed on the top tier bedrooms of the same, 2-story living unit as twelve to sixteen adolescent girls who occupied the lower tier bedrooms. One minute we had the boys constantly teasing the girls and the girls wanting to literally kill the boys to the next minute dealing with a love triangle and imaginary butterflies fluttering all over the place. It was an extreme test of our patience and skill to deal with boys with their developing testosterone and girls with their hormonal changes. They were all required to dine together, complete chores, and attend school and all other programs together. I'm sure you can imagine the deviousness, the mischief, and the chaos that ensued on any given day! Yet, I survived, and they survived...but it was not always fun!

Upon approaching the two-year mark of my return to the Centre, I became restless once again and began to search for a change – a new direction and career adventure that would challenge me. My unit's working conditions were not satisfactory to me either, and if I am not completely committed to how a situation stands, I find ways to change it. With a career shift in mind, I began to take advantage of as many supervisory and leadership courses and workshops offered by the Ministry as possible in preparation for my next career move. Furthermore, I started volunteering to take on additional, case management duties for the unit supervisor and covering his entire duties when he went on leave. This provided exposure to the special needs of various young offenders and the different personalities of unit staff, plus experience with the intertwining relationships with the other departments within the institution. I gained an abundance of relevant experience to include in my resume for the next available career move opportunity that presented itself.

However, my next career advancement did not come easy. Once again, I was told that the unit and the youth in my charge needed my strength and stability on the floor. Alas, I was apparently too good to be promoted!!!

Chapter 5

CAREER – INTERMEDIATE YEARS

In 1997, after I endured many interview rejections and second place placements (at least that's what I was always told when I sought feedback), the Calgary Young Offender Centre hired a new, progressive Director at its helm. This Director was different. She was proactive in her dealings with staff concerns and offender issues. She was fair with everyone and did not condone the cliques in the Centre that existed under her predecessor. Instead, hard work, commitment, and individual strengths in relation to the betterment of all staff and the entire Centre were appreciated and acknowledged by this Director. Her name was Karen Ferguson.

Karen may have been petite in stature, but her confidence and demeanor made her a huge presence wherever she went. She was incredibly intelligent, audacious, and fun. She was also habitually late – she operated on an African time zone mentality. Her laugh was so deep, hearty, and vibrant that it travelled miles ahead of her. She filled the space with her care and dedication.

The clique culture of the Centre began to change under the leadership of Director Karen Ferguson. The offenders were being offered more meaningful programs, the quiet youth were given a voice through the Youth Advisory Committee that was formed, and staff provided direct access to her office. Despite her role and responsibilities, she was always approachable.

Being a fair-minded lady with high energy and even higher integrity, Karen inspired, challenged, and motivated those around her. She definitely did this for me, plus she exposed me to many learning opportunities before she returned to Edmonton, her home city, to take over as the Director of the Edmonton Young Offender Centre. Soon after her return to Edmonton, Karen joined Alberta Human Services as the Assistant Deputy Minister in charge of Early Childhood and Community Supports Division. She championed a "Policy-Practice Conversation Focusing on Children and Youth with Complex Needs and Access to the Mental Health System" before retiring in 2014 after almost four decades of public service. Her dedication and genuine heart for making a difference made a deep impression on me and fueled my own desire for living a life of service.

During Karen's tenure as Director at CYOC, I applied and interviewed for yet another supervisory position at the Centre. I prepared intensely and diligently as always, leaving no stone unturned in my research and study for the position. As part of my preparation, I interviewed the young people we served as clients. My goal was to find out what they felt was missing or needed from their unit supervisor. In addition, I interviewed a select, cross-section of my colleagues to gauge what they looked for in a supervisor and what they thought was lacking at the time. I also interviewed current supervisors to find out the relationship and correlation between the duties of the supervisor to the total operations of the Centre and what impact this had. I wanted the big picture so that I would be ready for this new position interview.

Most of the people I talked with were very helpful. However, there was one individual whom I had long suspected of being a bully. This person was not fond of anybody that did not fit into his narrow, bigoted views, but I gave him a chance anyway...and he exposed himself. Rather than answering the job-related questions I asked him, he went on a long rant about how I was being "different and always speaking about my culture". I thanked him for his time and moved on.

In light of my interaction with this fellow, I felt like I had gotten some interesting insight. It appeared that, based on how things had gone and been run at the Centre in the past, this person's opinions had carried great weight all those times that I had placed "second" in interviews before. Being a different Director was at the helm of the decision-making this time, I was extremely optimistic about my chances.

The interview panel consisted of a Human Resources consultant and two Centre managers, one of them being Al

Ruttan, my Team Manager. I felt exceptionally good after the interview. I knew that I had done my homework well, and I particularly loved the rush I got when presenting myself in the interview. My days of literary and debating competition in high school had prepared me for such a time as this.

The announcement of the successful candidate took longer than expected...but I never lost hope. I later found out that there had been a split decision amongst the interview panel members. The story was that the Human Resource consultant and Al Ruttan had voted in favour of me as the successful candidate whereas the other manager, a member of the old boys' club and way of thinking, disagreed. The final decision, however, rested with Karen Ferguson who chose me as the new supervisor.

Although I very much expected to get the position, I was still somewhat shocked at the announcement. After experiencing so many previous rejections, enduring years of (attempted) bullying and degrees of discrimination, plus isolating work atmospheres, I had finally seen my perseverance and determination to push through the obstacles rewarded. I immediately called my husband in disbelief yet barely containable excitement. Until the official announcement was made, I couldn't discuss it with anybody at work. The rest of the day, I couldn't concentrate on my work, and the shift took forever to end. I eventually got home and indulged in a celebratory dance with much gratitude to the Almighty.

I was grateful for my resiliency in overcoming the many obstacles in my way up to this point. I deeply appreciated Karen Ferguson and the interview panel members who dared to be honest about my interview score. Because of my determination to make a difference and serve others well, I didn't settle for mediocrity but let grit and fortitude help propel me forward. The realization of this promotion coming to pass was an exceedingly great moment in my life.

This new position marked a milestone in more than one way. I was the only black, permanent staff member in the entire building of over one hundred personnel outside of one other employee – a male, Canadian-born, casual staff member. Also, I was the first black supervisor in the building and remained the only black supervisor for over twenty years.

Under Karen's directorship, the Centre expanded its connection and partnership within the City of Calgary and beyond. Karen encouraged me as a supervisor to reach beyond the gates of the Centre in partnership with agencies like: the Calgary Police Service, the City of Calgary Neighbourhood and Family Services, the Elizabeth Fry Society, the John Howard Society, Hull Homes, Woods Homes, the Parent Support Association of Calgary, Alberta Health Services – Adolescent Addictions and Mental Health programs, and more. She also provided opportunities for enhanced learning that I relished and enjoyed.

As an effective teacher and supervisor, every pertinent aspect of knowledge and education that I acquired through my contacts and training I shared with my staff for their own personal and professional growth and development. I love learning, and I enjoy sharing! I had earned this new supervisor position, but I truly appreciated the value of the expansion of knowledge I was given and the opportunities I had to improve myself. As I was given, I wanted to give back to those on my staff. Thus, I regularly provided learning and development opportunities to my staff, including one day a month when I would cover their shift while they attended any job-related event, such as a police ride-along, an anti-bullying conference, or a training on child abuse and the exploitation of minors. In return, I expected them to share their newfound knowledge and experiences with their colleagues during the next team meeting.

Occasionally covering for the staff on the unit allowed them some much-needed breathing space. It also demonstrated my leadership style – that of leading by example. Again, I set myself apart from the rest of the supervisors with how I treated and interacted with my staff.

My policy was to communicate my expectations clearly to my staff to avoid assumptions and misunderstandings. That is not to say that there weren't misunderstandings from time to time, but everyone knew what I stood for and the integrity behind my standards. Not only was I personally involved in the day-to-day operations of the unit, I made myself accessible to the youth and their legal guardians, as well as to the staff and service provider partners in and out of the Centre. My priorities framed my success as a supervisor, contributed to the personal growth of the young people on my unit, and aided the success and professional development of my staff.

Here is some feedback I received from a couple of my staff:

"From the first day of my career in Youth Justice, Moji acted as a mentor towards myself and many others. There were many times where Moji not only encouraged creativity in our work but also modeled this by using unique approaches that went against the ordinary. Thus, I learned to think outside the box and be a more effective mentor/figure in the lives of at risk and Justice involved youth. This creative approach was not always popular among all people involved, but Moji showed that she valued the process and went ahead and made bold decisions that challenged the way many would think. I am proud of the work I do and this is a trait that Moji instilled from the day I met her.

"Not only did Moji encourage a creative approach in our work, she also encouraged our own growth. Moji pushed staff to do work they may not have seen themselves capable of at the time, and the result was growth and personal development. The confidence Moji showed in staff, while providing support, provided opportunity for growth and an overall better experience at work for both the staff members and youth.

"I think it is fair to say that Moji had high expectations, and if you were willing to rise to those expectations, you would see yourself succeed. This success came with Moji supporting and cheering you on to be better. Moji also took time to share experiences that weren't only work related, and as a younger staff member starting out, these conversations were valued as growth was required on a personal level too! Moji also cared very much for the youth and was always an important advocate for them, which is something that I remember as I continue my career with this vulnerable population. To sum up the influence Moji has had, I would say she cheered you on to rise to her expectations and grow in work and life in general, but the amazing part is the expectations were higher than you may have had for yourself, and accomplishing such things felt good!

"Thank you, Moji, for believing in everyone and leaving your mark in Youth Justice that I carry with me as I continue my career."

Trevor Nash, Program Coordinator

"Moji Taiwo, an accomplished Deputy Director, a successful, real estate mogul, and a proud Mother and Wife, are words that would only be the beginning in describing Moji to anyone who hadn't (sic) had the pleasure of meeting her. I had the privilege of working for Moji for many years, and she had a significant impact on my growth, both personally and professionally. We shared a passion for real estate, and I will always remember the many conversations we had about it and the important life lessons that I learnt. Moji was a proud youth worker and supervisor, a worker whose passion and purpose was for helping others, and it was contagious. Although firm, and some would even describe as tough, she always had your best interest at heart, and she did whatever she could to ensure a better life for others!

"Thank you, Moji, and I wish you all the best in all of your future endeavours!"

Danny Gottlieb

Karen also appointed me as the chair of the Youth Advisory Committee. This committee provided the young people opportunities to have their voices heard and their concerns addressed in a collaborative, effective way. The advisory committee meetings allowed them to bring forward their issues but also enabled the exploration of possible solutions in a positive environment. It taught the kids how to present their problems, process them, and arrive at options that benefited the majority without compromising the integrity of the Centre's security. It was yet another chance for me to promote growth and maturity in their lives.

Twice yearly, from 1999 to 2009, I facilitated the instructional segment of the Life Skills Training Program of the Youth Worker Recruit Training at the Alberta Justice and Solicitor General Training Academy (staff college) in Edmonton. I taught recruits from young offender institutions across the province. Being able to pass along my knowledge and experience was just another way to give back, assisting others on their journeys of service within my Ministry.

Myles Anderson was the Director of the Grand Prairie Young Offender Centre and the Young Offender Training Program Coordinator at the Academy. After his retirement in 2002, I was assigned the training coordination position for the province's Young Offender (custody) Branch. Again, I was blessed with the opportunity to be a part of equipping others for civil service.

The responsibility as the coordinator in this capacity took me away from home for six weeks in the spring and in the fall each year. I drove back home every Friday night to be with my family on the weekend but then got back on the road again on Sunday afternoon to avoid driving in darkness. The three-hour, highway commute was dreadful when it snowed, especially when it was accompanied by icy road conditions and wind gusts between the towns of Bowden and Leduc. I was on my own on these drives and was often scared...but conversations with my Creator kept me alert, protected, and safe.

The City of Edmonton also receives a significant amount of snow in both winter and spring without the benefit of the warm, Chinook winds that are enjoyed in the southern part of the province including Calgary. Therefore, it became my regular routine while up in Edmonton to add thirty minutes to the start of my day to clear the snow off my vehicle and another half hour at the end of the day for the same reason.

While away from home, I was accommodated comfortably by a family friend of ours. Jerry Ojo lived on the west side of Edmonton and was close enough to the college that I didn't have to reside at the college residence. The college buildings had previously housed Catholic Nuns before the Government of Alberta purchased the buildings and the land. Imagine the living quarters of these nuns with hard, single beds, shared rooms, shared bathrooms, and common living and dining areas. It

141

reminded me of my stint at the General Hospital Student Residence where I lived in an old building with cold, damp rooms and strange, creepy noises, cold water taps producing scalding, hot water, and more inconveniences and discomforts. Not for me! Not again! I really appreciated Jerry's generosity in opening up his home where I had my own private and comfortable bedroom, a private bathroom, and the opportunity for quiet moments after a long day.

During my time as supervisor, I really challenged and enhanced my skills by enrolling in leadership, in-service training courses offered by the Ministry and through community partnership conferences. I took many courses that included the following: Interactive Leadership, Leading a Positive Work Place, Employee Relations for Government of Alberta Supervisors, Managing and Resolving Conflicts, Victims of Crime Protocol, Family Violence Recognition, Managing Performance through Coaching, Understanding Competencies in Learning and Development, and Curriculum Development for Adult Learning. Even though I had achieved the position I had, I didn't waste any opportunity to continue to learn so that I could serve those I interacted with daily in better and more effective ways.

Between 1997 and 2001, I also reported to the Assistant Director (also known as the Programs Director), a man by the name of Frank Vorstermans, and to a Deputy Director, who happened to be Barbara McKnight. Yes, this was the same Barb who was my first unit partner when I worked in Strathmore. As a unit supervisor, Frank oversaw my case management responsibilities while Barb oversaw my unit operational responsibilities. I had the pleasure of learning daily from two managers with distinct qualities and different leadership styles.

Through Frank's mentorship, I became proficient in policy and procedures application as well as dealing with the courts and legal aspects of my job. I really valued our candid discussions about life, too. Years later, he would play a major role in my career mobility.

From Barb, I gained more skill in the art of diplomacy when working with many staff with different personalities. I also learnt from her how to acknowledge good work openly but correct less acceptable work privately. This leadership approach works very well with almost anybody. I encourage you to try it sometime.

From 1997 to 2003, I enjoyed my position as a unit supervisor, moving among different units as needed but never leaving the female unit at CYOC. In the summer of 2002, I supervised three different units from one wing of the building to the opposite end of the building due to a chronic, absentee supervisor. Each unit consisted of six youth workers and an average of twenty young people. Suffice it to say, I was extremely busy that summer with the additional responsibilities that totaled almost sixty cases and eighteen staff. During that summer, I walked the halls from unit to unit, which gave me good body tone for I had no other time or extra energy to hit the gymnasium back then. With all that walking, I was exhausted by the time I got home.

Having to cover for that supervisor provided me the opportunity to demonstrate to my bosses my capabilities. Sadly, this person eventually lost his position after many years of attempts and support to hold him accountable. He was a nice man, and I was sad for him.

I couldn't help noting that, had it been me — a black, immigrant woman — who had been repeatedly absent for such prolonged and frequent periods of time, the system would not have been so accommodating for so long. First generation immigrants often endure many hardships and unfair treatment in the workplace largely due to the fear of reprisal if we speak up and/or a lack of awareness of our rights. It's highly unfortunate.

Despite the challenges of this time in my life, I enjoyed my many roles and the fast-paced nature of the work environment. My learning increased exponentially and my passion for sharing ignited. I thoroughly enjoyed passing along my skills to my staff, both experienced and newbies alike. In the same way, I was thrilled to learn from all the people around me as well.

Suddenly, it was announced that Karen Ferguson, my mentor, was moving on to greener pastures. Karen had accepted a new position in Edmonton. The majority of those who worked with her in Calgary genuinely missed her and her exceptional leadership.

With Karen's departure and another manager's retirement, there was a lot of management shuffling and realignment occurring in the building. Frank Vorstermans, who had been the Director of SYDC prior to its closure, was announced as the new Director, and Ramona Deer, my sister friend from our days at the North Haven Group Home, was promoted as the Programs Director.

At that point, I was very content with my stable, Monday to Friday, 8:30 a.m. to 4:30 p.m. days with the occasional late shift thrown in. And I always had the weekends and statutory holidays off. I took my vacation when my children had their summer off from school to maximize my family time. It was a far cry from those early days of shift work and childcare nightmares. Although the shift work back then allowed me to volunteer at my children's schools and enjoy three days off at a time, this regular and consistent shift came at a time when my children were in junior high, senior high, and university. This had its benefits, as we were all able to spend the evenings together as a family, either at home or at various, afterschool program venues.

However, with the new management shuffling going on due to Karen's and the other manager's departure, my stability was bound to be shaken whether I liked it or not. I could be moved to a Team Leader position with a rotational shift schedule, or minimally, I would most certainly be assigned a different manager to report to. I reported to Barb at that time, but looking at the pool of managers on the roster, I didn't believe that any of the other choices available were qualified enough people to be my new boss. In fact, one of them was the bully I referenced earlier who I had run up against while preparing for my supervisory interview! I had a decision to make – a decision that would impact my life in and out of the workplace, a decision that would influence my job satisfaction and quality of life, and a decision that would affect my family.

I discussed my dilemma with the only person who would be able to understand my predicament without being emotionally attached to my ultimate decision. Barb listened intently while I went through the scenarios I had been pondering in anticipation of the management job posting. At the end of my elaboration of the possible scenarios and their effects, she simply asked, "Moji, what are you going to do?"

The management job vacancies were finally posted, and I submitted my application the same day the posting came out. I did not tell my husband of my decision until I arrived home that night. Had I been faced with too much emotional and sentimental attachment with my having the weekends off, I probably would not have applied for the position. Instead, should I be one of the successful candidates, I would be going back to a rotational shift schedule that included night shifts that I had never worked before. It was either that or having to live with the high possibility of having to accept orders and take direction from that bully manager for the rest of my career. My choice was to return to a rotational shift schedule before I subjected myself to a work relationship that was demeaning in nature.

After submitting my application, I began to prepare for the interview as if my life depended on it. And in some ways, it *did* feel like my career life was on the line. From previous interview hurdles that I had faced, I did *not* want to leave this one to chance. If I couldn't rely on my interview performance alone to become a supervisor, I knew I couldn't rely on it alone now to secure this manager position.

I prepared diligently and with great intensity. My competencies and special contributions to the Young Offender Branch (YOB) and the Centre would have to be especially highlighted during this interview. I studied the Policy and Procedure Manual, reviewed my notes on Government of Alberta Employee Relations as well as the Bargaining Unit booklet. Since I already had expansive experience in education and the programming side of management, I became more familiar with the operational, security, and budgeting side of the

Centre. All this and more I did as preparation for this all-important interview.

Because I am a morning person, I had developed a habit of scheduling my interviews for the morning, preferably with me being the first interview candidate of the day. Not only am I fresh and able to set the pace for the other candidates, the panel members also get to hear original answers from me before it becomes redundant hearing it from many other candidates. Additionally, I could carry on with the rest of my day and be more relaxed as the pressure of the interview for me was over while others were still feeling stressed waiting for their interview times later in the day.

I was very confident going into the interview, but I couldn't imagine how the stars would align in my favour. Then, I walked into the boardroom. The sight of the panel members immediately energized me. There was a Human Resources consultant who was a woman of East African heritage on the panel. The Executive Director of the Young Offender Branch, Kevin O'Brien, was present. I had worked with him briefly at SYDC and had traded stories with him about immigrants' struggles as his wife and her parents had emigrated from Tanzania. Finally, there was my Centre Director, Frank Vorstermans, who also, with his parents and brother, emigrated from the Netherlands. Frank arrived in Canada as a six-year-old child without knowing a word of English. He had shared with

148

me before the struggles he endured in school, which gave him greater empathy towards immigrant children. Frank was also a mentor and a coach to whom I had shared many of my workplace unfairness concerns and frustrations. His advice to me had been to not lose focus and to believe in my abilities. I sat down for my interview knowing that two out of the three panel members could verify all my assertions. Only the Human Resources consultant needed convincing. I could do this!

I felt extremely positive after the interview and eagerly awaited the result. In the meantime, the building was abuzz with rumours, innuendoes, and opinions about all the candidates, especially about me having the nerve to think that I could aspire to this management level. I was not bothered in the least. Rather, I focused on my job and went about my daily business as usual. I was confident in who I was and in my capabilities to take on any challenge. Besides, I knew I had nothing to lose for trying...but I would have lost a great deal more if I had never tried at all.

Chapter 6

TRIALS TO TRIUMPHS

From an early age, my mother often told me that no life was without its challenges. However, she also emphasized that how resourceful a person was would determine how successful they would be in seeking resolutions to those challenges. Some of the inner resources needed to take on the challenges of life are one's strengths and resiliency, clear vision and self-assurance, and kindness and humility.

Challenges in My Early Life

From the age of thirteen to eighteen, I attended a co-ed boarding school in a different state from where I was born and raised. Because I started school very young as a gangly four-year-old, I completed my elementary school years early. I obviously was ready for learning and smart enough, even back then.

As I was determined not to attend high school in my home city and state, I had to delay my high school entrance by one year to afford my parents the time and opportunity to raise the necessary funds to pay for my school tuition and fees, lodging and transportation, books, along with other miscellaneous expenditures. My parents were older, and with me being the seventh of eight children, scraping together the funds wasn't easy as most of their resources were stretched thin.

Like my siblings, I had been working since age six. My mother ran a confectionary store and sold anything and everything in season from non-perishable goods and canned foods, to fruits, kola nuts, and so on. Every day after school, I would have a quick snack, complete my homework, and then it would be time to go to different neighbourhoods to sell whatever products she had arranged on a tray for me. She would itemize the goods with their prices and include a summary of the total amount I had to bring back home after everything was sold. I'd memorize all the prices in addition to the amount of petty cash she would give to me to make change. Nothing was written down, and all had to be accounted for at the end of the day. Through this repeated exercise, I learnt to balance my account at a very young age.

It was amazing how Mother always assumed that I was going to sell everything. I think that was her way of applying pressure on me, although a subtle one, to earn my commission through this challenge. My "pay" was usually a word of praise or a piece of candy that I was not to eat but expected to sell for my reward. None of us kids *dared* to eat the candies!

My mother never accounted for the fact that I would most likely run into other kids my age, kids who *didn't* have to work and who had plenty of time to play. Naturally, I was tempted to join in and have fun. When I did, I often *totally* forgot the time...and then panic would set in.

In addition to this responsibility to sell goods, my mother was extremely strict, and I was given a specific timeframe to return home with all the money I had made from selling my items. You know what they say: time goes fast when you're having fun! Most times, I lived up to my mother's expectations of being a pro at peddling the goods entrusted to me. At times, however, I put pleasure before peddling, giving in to the distraction of playing with other kids...and I wouldn't sell as much. It was during times like these that I'd visit my older sisters' shops for redemption. These siblings took turns purchasing my goods whether they wanted to or not in order to help me out, sending me home with the correct amount of money for my mother. Their generosity spared me from experiencing my mother's whipping rod for slacking on the job. I am so grateful and indebted to my sisters for their kindness to me during those times.

As the years went by, I desperately wanted to put an end to my peddling career. As a preteen girl, I felt humiliated in front of my friends in having to do this job. To the disappointment of my mother, who had come to depend on my abilities to assist her, I chose to go to a boarding school. She relented, for she was also a strong advocate of education, but she promised not to come and visit me while I was away.

Therefore, almost as a parting gift, my mother would repeat those words – that no life was without its challenges, but how resourceful a person was would determine how successful they would be in seeking resolutions to those challenges. Every time I came home on school breaks she would remind me. Every time it was time to return to school for another semester of having to look after myself, she would repeat it. She drilled this principle into me relentlessly for five years.

At the end of my year at home after completing elementary school, I was enrolled at Ebenezer Grammar School in Iberekodo, Abeokuta. Abeokuta is the largest city in Ogun State, which is located in the southwestern region of Nigeria. My boarding school was situated on an expansive, fenced-in acreage with many educational buildings and living quarters on the property. All our daily activities were held on campus with an outing day once a month where we could venture into the city for shopping or just hang out with friends.

The driving distance from Lagos to Abeokuta is approximately 100 kilometers, taking about one hour through private transportation. When schools were out for breaks and holidays, there were many students from different schools in the city heading in a multitude of directions to visit their family homes elsewhere. It was often chaotic but also exhilarating to ride on public transit with its many stops in between. I'm sure it took at least three hours to arrive at our destinations when taking public transit.

True to her word, my mother didn't visit me once while I was away at school, although I would have given my right arm for a single visit from her. Nonetheless, I felt her presence, mainly through those constant words reminding me about the challenges of life. I reacted mostly out of fear at that time, but as I grew older, I came to realize that she believed in me, and she knew I could take care of myself. She had equipped me with all the necessities of self-sufficiency either through her words or through practical training growing up like my peddling job. Nevertheless, it was harsh to witness other students receive visits from their families on visiting days but not me. To keep myself busy, I spent my visiting periods either reading or doing sports.

My father visited me once, and I remember how surprised and elated I was the time he came. Because I resemble my father most, many of my schoolmates who saw him at the entrance gate to the school grounds suspected that he was my father, and they ran to inform me that I had a visitor. Of course, I didn't believe them. I was already midway through my high school years with no visit to date. Wondering who could be there to see me, I hurried cautiously towards the visiting hall

155

with an entourage of curious schoolmates...and there was my father! We embraced ecstatically, and I cried with joy. For my schoolmates to have recognized him without having met him before, I just felt like that was incredible, too. That visit was one of the highlights of my boarding school years!

My mother's words sustained me throughout boarding school and beyond. They have proven to have great impact on how I have been able to identify my strengths and shortcomings, as well as my wants, needs, and fears. They have influenced how I've analyzed and approached my contributions to humankind. As I've dealt with both the joys and challenges of my service towards others, they have enlarged my pool of human resources that have, in turn, aided me (and continue to aid me) in tackling some of the trials in my path. As a result, I have learnt how to transform my trials into triumphs. My mother's wise words have shaped my views on challenges, and I don't see problems. Instead, I see possibilities.

More Challenges

I have faced challenges from the moment I emigrated to Canada. When I arrived in Calgary in the freezing, cold winter and saw no familiar face to welcome me to my new country, my survival instincts manifested, and my mother's words kicked me into action. With the grace of God, rather than being frozen with panic, I used the initial panic of the situation to ignite my ability to search out ways to take care of myself. This led to the self-confidence and determination I had in approaching more than one person to help me resolve the problem of tracking down my brother. And because I was brave enough to step out and not give up or give in to panic, that one moment of initial disappointment led to three acts of kindness that very first day of my immigrant's journey.

I have faced challenges in pursuing higher education. For one, I had desperately wanted to attend the Journalism program at Southern Alberta Institute of Technology (SAIT) but was not given admission because of my accent. However, by keeping my options open, I was able to attend the Lethbridge Community College (LCC), now simply known as Lethbridge College. There, I was fortunate to meet supportive instructors like Ian Mandin (RIP) and Georgia Fooks who encouraged me in my quest for higher education and were not put off by my accent. Additionally, I could live with my husband instead of being separated for the two-year duration of being enrolled in a SAIT program. The challenge of coming up against discrimination because of my accent indirectly led me to the open door of furthering my education at the University of Lethbridge and obtaining my degree.

Part of being successful is recognizing that a closed door is sometimes the best thing that could happen to you. In

Lethbridge, I began a career with the Government of Alberta that spanned over three decades and brought about my family's ultimate return to Calgary where we have since flourished in all aspects of our lives. On the other hand, there would have been many sacrifices attached to being a successful journalist had I been able to take that route, especially as a female. It would have involved a lot of travelling and absences from home in the early days of my career, which is not often conducive to having a family or maintaining a stable family home. Since my first daughter arrived, creating and maintaining a stable family unit became extremely important to me. I was able to achieve that stability with my change of career path. Not bad for a girl turned down and rejected for SAIT's Journalism program by the renowned reporter and news anchor, Darryl Janz!

It would've been easy to focus on the struggles to achieve success in post-secondary pursuits and miss the joys that came alongside those trials. Many of those joys came in the form of people connections that made a difference. I met my college best friend, Connie Watson, and other angel friends like Lynda Harris, Gloria Haddow (RIP), and Mitch Bechtold. In every situation, there's the possibility to make meaningful connections or to discover other environments where such connections can be found. Remember the winter when my husband and I were forced out of our studio apartment because of our skin colour? If you recall, we got no assistance from the police officer either. However, the incident gave us an opportunity to explore other living arrangements and ultimately secure a newer, better living space with wonderful landlords and neighbours. The joys of meaningful relationships can be found if you are willing to look for and embrace them.

The confrontation with discrimination and mistreatment through that landlady, as unfair and inhumane as it was, made us realize a few other things as well. We discovered that we had settled for less and paid much more than we should have paid for the apartment. The crisis of being kicked out in the middle of winter led us to search out better and fairer options. Furthermore, the experience also encouraged us to learn more about the Landlord and Tenancy Act and what our rights were as tenants. Finally, it gave us an incentive to own our home, which we pledged to purchase as soon as we could afford it. We bought our first home in 1985 and followed up with the purchase of a rental property in 1986 with many more purchases years later. Subsequently, we created a real estate, investment holding company that we still operate to this day. Due to our previous negative experience, we made it our mission to always treat our tenants fairly. Sometimes, the opportunity we have within a difficult or tough situation where we are treated badly is to determine within that moment that we are going to *be* different and thus *make* a difference. Our personal gestures in that regard toward our tenants have been appreciated by most, often resulting in long-term friendships.

Building My Career

Once my post-secondary education was done, I faced the challenges of full-time employment and building my career. After eagerly accepting my first, major job offer, I faced one of my first, career-related hurdles when I found out I was being underpaid by my employer. This taught me a valuable lesson, which was, and still is, to always take time to review documents and to seek clarification when in doubt. The challenge of learning from my own oversight and lack of awareness was used to benefit my dealings in the future.

Next, I was passed over for promotion at Strathmore Youth Development Centre (SYDC) because "I was needed more on the floor". This incident could have held me back...had I let it. Instead, upon realizing that my hard work would not be rewarded, I made a bold move and decided that my best chance for progress would be to leave the team at SYDC for the opportunity at the North Haven Group Home. When the group home closed months later, instead of it being another setback (as some may have viewed it), it cleared a path for me to move on to the Calgary Young Offender Centre (CYOC). After I had settled into routine at CYOC and was busy gaining valuable

160

experience moving between various positions, SYDC was forced to close, leaving many of the staff who were left there with few opportunities to choose from regarding which Centre they wanted to be reassigned to. Some of them even got demoted so that they could be accommodated at CYOC. I had dodged the bullet! Rather than settling for the frustrations that I had been dealing with at SYDC, I chose to make changes that resulted in my ending up in a Centre of my own choosing and with better prospects moving forward. In addition, transferring to CYOC before the closure of SYDC also factored prominently in my husband's and my decision to purchase a home in a new sub-division in the city closer to the Centre, a property that has tripled in value since its purchase and added to our real estate, wealth-building program. One frustrating obstacle, when viewed as an opportunity to make positive changes, led to many beneficial outcomes.

While the move to CYOC exposed me to more overt discrimination and outright racism, it also provided me with greater insight into how to identify and form alliances with people who had my back and believed in my capabilities. I was familiar with racial jokes disguised as humour, like when a manager at SYDC asked me about the dark spots on my face. I responded to him that they were freckles. Thinking it a joke, he laughed, pointed, and announced, "Those aren't freckles! Black people don't have freckles!" I could have let discrimination and racism, even under the guise of a joke, define me. However, I let these incidences focus me into seeking out and making those meaningful connections that were not tainted by narrow-minded opinions and viewpoints.

Every job comes with its drawbacks and issues. Yet, there are also advantages within each job, especially if you have the eyes to see and the resolve to seek them out. At CYOC, despite the discrimination and racism I faced, I also had a greater pool of positive people to align with. In addition, I had many more opportunities to move around within and outside of the Centre, permitting me to expand my connections even more. I changed unit placements to gain wider exposure to different offender populations and different unit partners and supervisors to add to my repertoire of experiences and skill set. I moved to the Programs department, which allowed me to really spend quality, rehabilitative time with offenders. This ultimately led to the coordination of the Alternative Measures Program that I facilitated in the community. After a four-year stint as the Alternative Measures Coordinator, I became a Unit Supervisor and Team Leader a few months after my return to the Centre, a situation that came with its own set of challenges. Regardless of the obstacles I faced though, there were always opportunities available to me.

Management Challenges

Once I returned to CYOC and resumed my unit position, I faced a major challenge. There had been an economic downturn in the country and a recruitment freeze by the Government of Alberta during the period I had left the unit to oversee the Alternative Measures Program. My position had been filled with temporary staff until I came back. On my return to the team and my unit, my new unit partner was a guy who had not worked on the unit previously when I was there. However, I knew him as one of the bullies in the Centre.

Angus[6] was an older, British man who was hired on as a temporary, contract, youth worker, not because of his education or his care for the teenagers we served. Rather, he was hired (in my opinion) because he was a British, white male with boot camp experience for troubled teens.

The first day I stepped back onto the unit to begin my shift, this man fumed, grumbled, and was hostile with the residents throughout the shift. Once the youth were down for the night, I attempted to connect with him on a partnership level to establish a working frame and dialogue, to get to know each other, and to set out expectations and parameters as individuals and as a team. Well! I was in for a shock! Angus started to

---

[6] Name changed to protect identity

berate me for him having to lose his young, white, female, and timid partner due to me resuming my former role at CYOC. He also went after higher management in his rant, which at that time included Team Manager Barb McKnight and Centre Director Karen Ferguson. My shock did not stop at Angus's behaviour, but it was compounded by the support he received from what I perceived as the majority of the team members. This was a casual, temporary, staff employee giving me, a permanent, staff member, serious flak for returning to my rightful position. No non-white, male or female immigrant worker would have dared to display such deplorable behaviour without severe consequences. I was absolutely appalled at his conduct!

I allowed Angus time to exhaust himself before I laid down the rule under which we both would work together. I made it abundantly clear to him that, under no circumstances, would he address me in such a manner again. Furthermore, if he continued to badmouth Barb and Karen, I would personally repeat everything he had said about these women to them while he was present. This was to be the basis of our work partnership.

Angus was never antagonist towards me again. I had laid down the law and established proper boundaries with regard to his dealing with me early on, but his words continued to be brutal with the female residents we worked with. Finally, I had

had enough of his awful conduct and continued harsh treatment and abuse of the young people under our care. After observing that this man was in no way going to change or improve in his treatment of others, I informed him in no uncertain terms that I would make sure that he was removed from that unit. And he was. We both parted ways, and I became Unit Supervisor for the unit a few months later.

Within a few weeks of my promotion, I started to reorganize the unit by holding staff meetings, outlining clear, programming goals for us as a team and for the residents. Practicum students were included in these meetings as part of their learning plans. Creating a strong, team environment has always been important to me and has proven to be a critical component to my success.

Unbeknownst to me at the time, another challenge was brewing. There was a practicum student on the unit that happened to be Angus's protégé. Apparently, she had reported to him that comments had been made on the unit, particularly ones allegedly made by me, that she felt were offensive towards him.

Angus immediately initiated my first trial as a supervisor. Taking offence at this second-hand information, he was convinced that, as a union member and a subordinate, he could mount a formal complaint against me for defamation of character. Proceeding, he filed the complaint at the highest level possible, bypassing all the established steps and procedures in place for initially dealing with such incidents. It became obvious that he was determined to destroy my career.

I received a call on my days off from Barb notifying me that the Centre Director had informed her of an impending investigation against me. She did not know who the investigators would be nor did she know when it would be. Naturally, the rest of my days off were extremely stressful because, while I knew that Angus did not like me and the feeling happened to be mutual, I couldn't think of anything that would have caused him to want to disrupt my recent achievement so drastically...unless he was still sore about my role in getting him transferred out of my unit and was seeking revenge. However, if that was the case, where did the accusation of defamation of character fit in? I hadn't taken any of our confrontations public at all. In fact, I couldn't recall any public altercation that could have been interpreted as an attack on his character. If anything, I should have been the one to file a complaint against him for his attempts at harassment when I returned to my position. My mind was going a mile a minute with this development.

The investigators would be comprised of people from another branch along with union representatives. I had never faced anything like this before, and the one-week wait until I faced this "firing squad" felt like a century. In the meantime, rumours abounded in the Centre, and Angus walked around like a peacock strutting amongst his cohorts.

The investigation was conducted, many people were interviewed, and I waited nervously for the outcome. I didn't know whom the culprit was who had taken a distorted report of me to Angus, and I didn't know who was on my side, who wasn't, and in whom I could trust. It was an exceedingly anxious and stressful time.

Finally, two weeks later, I was informed that I had been cleared of all the allegations against me. Furthermore, there would be no demerits from the complainant placed in my records. In addition, almost simultaneously, a student placement on my unit was terminated, and for the first time, I knew who had been behind the allegations. Truth had prevailed! I had survived another challenge!

A few months later, I learnt that the investigators had interviewed all my unit staff members and a selection of the unit residents and had discovered that Angus's claim was very much to the contrary. In fact, all those people who had been afraid to stand up to Angus's terrible conduct and abusive ways before spoke out on my behalf when it really mattered. Through the investigation, Angus was exposed as the true bully. At that time, it baffled me how such a person could have gotten away with such flagrant intimidation and verbal abuse of residents and young female staff without repercussion. However, in the end, his unethical behavior ultimately led to his downfall.

That whole experience taught me the importance of being keenly aware of my surroundings and the people that occupy those spaces. It also affirmed my belief in exhibiting fairness and kindness to all people, regardless of who they are. For me in this situation, those who I had treated nicely spoke out loudly in my absence leading to my vindication. And this incident wasn't the only time that my good character and reputation withstood attempts by a few unscrupulous individuals in the workplace trying to derail my achievements and undermine my integrity.

As I continued as Unit Supervisor, I had the pleasure of working with some creative, hardworking, and caring, young staff on different units. Many of these employees had relocated from other provinces to Alberta in search of better opportunities. They truly appreciated a job when they got one, hence their dedication.

Unfortunately, among these brilliant people, there were always at least one or two individuals who operated with a sense of entitlement whose sole purpose on the job appeared to be one of social affiliation. One such person was Natalie[7]. At the time Natalie was hired, I was overseeing two units – the female unit and a unit where the most serious, male offenders

---

[7] Name changed to protect identity

in the province were housed. Natalie was one of the staff members employed on the male unit.

Natalie dressed well, which I truly appreciated. Personally, I love being well put together and respected that in others. As a young, single woman, she was friendly and flirtatious with male staff in the building, but I didn't expect her to extend that to the male young offenders on the unit. That was my first warning sign that something was off.

Gradually, I noticed that certain items that were prohibited in the Centre were showing up on her unit, and these items were generally discovered after her shifts. The matter was addressed at unit meetings a few times since nobody knew how the offenders were obtaining items not sold in the Centre's canteen. Still, the items continued to surface, but I couldn't find any solid evidence that Natalie was involved.

Meanwhile, Natalie's dresses and skirts gradually rose above her knees to the point of it becoming a legitimate concern for me. The nature of her job required her to regularly conduct physical searches of the residents and the facilities. Also, as a female, it was important for her to exhibit a positive and professional demeanor and dress, especially on the male unit. On the rare occasions that I worked late, I also observed that a certain, male offender got more attention than the rest, particularly during quiet and chore times on the unit. As a result, I began to suspect Natalie's relationship with this young man was more than a professional one with the proper boundaries, and my concerns were shared with my unit manager. Together, we both decided that the matter was serious enough that it needed to be addressed with Natalie.

Being as Natalie was a casual employee hoping to secure a permanent position, one would think she would have heeded the initial caution I gave her. Instead, she turned the matter into a popularity war against me. She told all her cohorts in the Centre, including some managers and the Program Director, about my discussion with her, twisting the facts to make it sound like I was attacking her personally. Consequently, she was encouraged to file a complaint with the union against me, which she subsequently did.

I continued to press management to address my concerns about Natalie dressing so provocatively on the units. Information came out that she had been a waitress in one of the bars that many of the male staff and the Program Director frequented. There, her skimpy dress was definitely appreciated by all the male patrons. Her popularity among the guys appeared to have a direct correlation to her approval to being hired to work at the Centre and the lack of objection to her attire.

While the matter continued to be investigated, one of the male offenders was suspected of having a romantic connection with Natalie. He had since turned 18 years old and completed his sentence and thus was released into the community. Unfortunately, he soon committed another crime as an adult while on probation. It was during his booking process that it was discovered that the offender was residing with Natalie. Furthermore, through further investigation, it was discovered that my suspicions were indeed valid – Natalie *had* been sexually involved with a few male offenders, including the newly arrested, young man who had been living with her. Her complaint against me was immediately dismissed, and she was terminated for breaching employment policy. Again, truth prevailed.

Back on the female unit, there was another female employee, Jessica[8], who was originally from the night shift working on a trial assignment with my team. This woman was skilled with the gift of gab. She could tell anybody what he or she wanted to hear, but I personally insisted on action to back up her words. Now, I expected my staff to develop weekly, program plans for their team, and Jessica had the habit of just copying what other teams had developed. I didn't mind that part so much *if* the program had been effectively delivered...but the problem was that Jessica was unable to deliver. Instead, she made up multiple excuses to leave the unit during program periods. It was also observed and reported by other Centre staff

---

[8] Name changed to protect identity

that Jessica frequented their male units too often and disrupted their programs. A few months passed, and all the supervisory efforts to assist Jessica were fruitless, and I recommended that she be returned to her night duties.

In November 2003, soon after Jessica's departure from my unit, I became a manager. I was on my first set of night shifts when I saw Jessica again, and she was once again a member of my team. She avoided me, but as a manager, I was responsible for my team members regardless of their personal feelings towards me.

The first few shifts were uneventful, but it wasn't long before I started noticing a familiar pattern. I strongly suspected Jessica was spending time visiting a male unit while on "bathroom breaks", leaving her assigned female unit and being regularly absent. Well, since I am not a person to ignore my instincts or potential warning signs, I shared my observation with her immediate supervisor who reported to me.

Though her supervisor followed up with Jessica, I couldn't be sure in what context. Since most of the older staff were white males at the time, they didn't expect nor did they accept a female, black person to be their manager, and I wasn't guaranteed that they would take my concerns seriously or not. Regardless of the manner in which Jessica was addressed, instead of accepting the cautionary feedback, she immediately filed a harassment complaint against me.

172

An investigation was initiated and, like before, went on for what seemed like an eternity. I began to ask myself why it was that other people got promoted and could enjoy the glory of their hard work and achievement for a while before facing major challenges often associated with their positions. Why was it that I barely got my toe in the river before I was being swept away by some difficulty or crisis? What was it about me that was contributing to my struggles? I seriously started to doubt myself. As a result, I spent countless hours soul searching and reviewing my own conduct and practices. In doing so, I reached the conclusion that I was holding myself accountable before anyone else had to, and I was indeed on the right track. I could be confident in my integrity as a professional.

The union investigation dragged on, and even though I had gone through self-examination to make sure that I was operating at the highest standards, it was nerve-wracking nonetheless. It didn't help that, throughout the interrogation, Jessica's supervisor, who I had asked to address my concerns with her, neither confirmed nor denied the harassment claim. Eventually, the complaint was found to be unsubstantiated and was dismissed.

Unfortunately, that wasn't the end of it. Jessica then escalated her complaint against me by taking it to the Alberta Human Rights Commission. She also claimed that she was too stressed to work because of me and the whole situation, and therefore was placed on paid, stress leave while the complaint continued to be investigated at a higher level.

Then while Jessica was on paid leave, her car was stopped for erratic driving by a city police cruiser. Naturally, the car's registration was run through the motor vehicle database to confirm ownership...but it wasn't Jessica driving. The person behind the wheel was none other than the young, male offender that I had suspected Jessica had been spending an unusual amount of time with when she was leaving her assigned unit during excessive bathroom breaks. Her case against me began to unravel.

Like with Natalie, Jessica was found to be romantically involved with a minor who was and had been in custody. In fact, it came out that she was actually living with this young offender and had aided him to violate the law while on probation as she had allowed him to drive her car without a driver's license. With this new development, Jessica incurred a charge of her own under the Criminal Code of Canada...and the human rights claim against me was dismissed.

My Creator, who had gifted me with instincts and foresight and developed within me self-discipline and exemplary work ethic, had done it again. The truth had prevailed. I was vindicated and my good character proven.

On reflection of this case, I stand by the fact that I had my concerns documented at the onset even though my reports based on my written records of what was going on caused me initial grief due to these disgruntled employees' reactions. As a result, I was spared having to squirm under an intense police investigation as a unit supervisor and team manager who did not report her suspicions in a timely manner.

Like Angus's allegation in my first week as a supervisor, Jessica's human rights complaint was filed within the first month of my management assignment. While this totally stressed me out, I was not deterred. I knew I was doing the right thing, and I was not going to compromise my principles in order not to ruffle any feathers.

I have always been an avid note taker. I had documented everything (and still do), but each of these management challenges further encouraged me to write everything down in detail. Chances are, I may forget minor details...but my notebook always remembers.

I also learnt that not everyone has my back when the going gets tough. Because of these allegations and investigations, the pool of loyal team members narrowed and got thinner as I climbed the corporate ladder. Yet, I have no regrets! Maintaining my integrity was what was important.

Dealing with Bullies

In my career, I have had to deal with bullies at one point or another. Kyle[9] was another fellow who worked at CYOC who became known for his excessive, bullying ways. He was extremely intolerant or racist towards those he felt were inferior or different, and he exhibited an arrogant, know-it-all attitude at all times. It was incredibly hard to deal with him. Although I had learnt to handle him mostly by ignoring him or responding with more intelligent answers when appropriate, it was very difficult to work alongside this man and endure his abuses.

Unbeknownst to me, he had been terrorizing another colleague of mine, a female manager named Bobbi[10], because of her sexual orientation. Apparently, Kyle and Bobbi had worked together for over twenty years in the Adult Offender Branch of our Ministry before they both joined the Young Offender Branch. Kyle arrived first, then Bobbi. During all those years of working together, he had ceaselessly made rude and demeaning comments to her until she finally reached a breaking point one day while working at our Centre.

Kyle's belittling antics came to a screeching halt one afternoon...but not before I was emotionally sideswiped. I was

---

[9] Name changed to protect identity
[10] Name changed to protect identity

scheduled to work an afternoon shift from 3:00 p.m. to 11:00 p.m., but I received a call early in the morning to report at the Centre for 1:00 p.m. for an emergency meeting. I had no idea what was up but wasn't initially concerned.

I strolled into the building with my usual cheerfulness and a grin on my face, only to be faced by a panel of executive investigators. "Uh oh! What have I done now?" I thought with apprehension. They must have read the panic on my face for they spoke gently and assuredly that they just wanted to ask me some questions, as they narrated that there had been a bullying complaint made by Bobbi against Kyle. Apparently, she had provided my name as a person that may have endured the same abuse and could corroborate her allegations.

Without uttering a single word, I started to sob uncontrollably. I attempted to talk but no words came out. Instead, the table was covered with a pool of my tears.

One of the investigators went out of the boardroom and came back with a box of tissues and a glass of water for me. They all sat there patiently while I cried. Occasionally, they told me to take time to collect myself and then let them know when I was ready to answer their questions.

All the memories of being directly and indirectly discriminated against and treated inhumanely flooded my heart and overwhelmed my emotions. My tough exterior – the shell I had enveloped myself with – cracked in that vulnerable moment.

The intensity of what I had been under throughout the years culminated in that one moment.

Once I regained my composure, my tale of mistreatment, unfairness, and blatant bigotry in the workplace poured out like a rainstorm, leaving the panel with bewildered looks on their faces.   I had vivid recollections of Kyle's inappropriate comments and indignations directed at me that I recounted to the investigators. The meeting lasted for over two hours, but it felt much longer. By the time it was concluded, I was too emotionally drained to join my team and was excused from my evening shift.

I felt like a weight of over twenty years had lifted off of me through finally being able to share the truth of what I had endured, getting that burden off my shoulders. Yet although I felt relieved, I was also sad. Kyle, on the other hand, was sanctioned for his conduct and immediately transferred to another institution.

This challenge took a while to work through as many challenges do. My resiliency in being able to recover from the hardships life inevitably brings is what held me in good stead all those years I faced unfair treatment. And it was my resiliency of heart and mind that helped me rise above this emotional crisis and move on in the knowledge that my humanity and the decency that was due me had finally been recognized.

Modeling Success

Since my high school days, I have been a "fashionista". I have always been photogenic and love to have my picture taken. In those early days of my career while at SYDC, I had received numerous compliments about my looks from various people, but I didn't pay too much attention to them at first. Believing in myself, I decided to utilize my good looks and love of the camera to pursue modeling as a paid hobby, which I still do even to this day.

Remember that manager who ridiculed my looks through his racist joking in an attempt to bring me down? Something like that can cause people to view themselves through a skewed lens. However, I resolved to do something that proved I was not going to let one person's negative perspective of my looks define my worth and value or diminish my natural beauty. Modeling gave me an avenue to show that I was not affected by such attacks.

My venture into modeling started when a segment of my Life Skills program for the female offenders turned into a fundraising fashion show at SYDC. I, along with Kathy Matthews (a Centre volunteer on my unit at the time), decided to hold make-up application and grooming classes. In preparation for the weekly classes, we needed to access the professional and product resources required to run the classes. Kathy introduced me to Delmar College of Hair and Esthetics. I inquired about and secured a volunteer student from the school to come and commit to our weekly sessions as part of her school training. During the sessions, along with the girls I worked with, I collected tips on appropriate makeup applications, coloring, and blending. Through the school, hair care and design were also incorporated into the program. The girls loved it!

To capture and celebrate all that had been learnt, the girls and I decided to host a fashion show. To assist us with the show as far as wardrobe, runway struts, and stage preparation, Kathy linked me to somebody at the (then) John Casablancas Modeling Agency in Calgary. The Life Skills class had exploded into a full-blown, Centre-wide production attended by the residents' families, staff, and representatives from the town of Strathmore.

I took to the runway for the first time with all the girls, led the way for them, and cheered them on. The girls were excited and fearless, and the positive attention they received in return for all their efforts was something most of them had never gotten before. All of them experienced a sense of accomplishment for all their hard work and were affirmed in

180

believing in themselves. For some of them, the program and culminating fashion show even birthed an interest in pursuing a career in makeup and hair artistry from that point on. As for me, at the end of the event, I was invited to sign on with the agency as a model. There began my part-time modeling career.

There weren't many black people in the city back then, and there were certainly very few black people who dared to venture onto such a platform as modeling in 1987. I didn't let that stop me. Soon after I began modeling, I entered the Mrs. Calgary Beauty Pageant contest hosted by Patti Falconer of Patti Falconer Modelling Agency. The contest generated a pool of approximately thirty, beautiful housewives and professional women, only two of which were black. After a few rounds of rigorous interviews and photo shoots, the list was scaled down to ten finalists...and I was one of them! There was a write up in the Calgary Sun along with pictures of the finalists, and I instantly became a local celebrity receiving congratulatory calls (and some weird/creepy ones, too) as well as adulations from my community and work colleagues. I ended up being the third runner-up at the finals, but that was just fine. I had accomplished what no other black woman had attempted before in the City of Calgary!

I wasn't prepared for the potential benefits that presented themselves as a result of this public, modeling exposure. My success led to the push to jump into the professional modeling world by either moving my family or leaving them for extended periods to pursue modeling in bigger markets like Toronto or Vancouver. A few opportunities came knocking from Vancouver, but I had a growing career already, small children at home, and a husband, and I wasn't prepared to disrupt our lives for a career in modeling. They were, and still are, more important to me. Therefore, I chose to stay closer to home and continue on the main career path I was already on.

This exposure in front of the camera led to other opportunities as well. Along with my three, little kids in tow, we auditioned for and appeared in both print and television commercials and as extras in films and television shows shot in and around Calgary. Consequently, my children started making their own money through show business. At an early age, they were set up with their own bank accounts and learnt important lessons in savings. Teaching them money management long before they started delivering flyers to the neighbourhood was very important to me, and I am proud to say that, as adults, my children are financially astute and independent. In addition, I believe the experience had a positive influence on my children. My son, Deji, and my second daughter, Adejoke, still model on the side as a paid hobby. In addition, Adejoke appeared on Project Runway Canada Season 2 and is a Fashion and Costume Designer who has worked on films and television series. Her young son also models from time to time. That manager who criticized my looks probably thought his put-down comments would have demoralized me, or at the very least, put me in my place as someone inferior. Rather, it propelled me to step forward and acknowledge those who had commented positively on my unique looks, use it to my advantage, embrace my beauty in a creative way, and ultimately pass down a legacy of self-confidence to my children that has contributed to their own successes.

In 2010, Sharon Cornwall of Fashion Has No Borders in collaboration with Ben Barry Agency put out a broadcast in search of women to enter the "Every Woman" Competition. One of my children entered me in the competition. Initially, I was reluctant to participate thinking that my modeling days were over. My one daughter reminded me that she had never seen me shy away from challenges or adventures before. With this reminder, I decided to investigate the criteria further.

As soon as I found out the criteria for the competition — individuality, confidence, charitable contirbutions, beauty, and inner strength — I decided to embrace the challenge and have fun while at it. I love having fun regardless of what I'm doing. Choosing to have fun is a deliberate choice I make even when facing challenges.

I entered the contest, and on March 20th, the final day of the search and competition, I was chosen the winner of Fashion Has No Boarders! I beat out hundreds of strong, intelligent, beautiful women of all shades, shapes, and talents. Part of the winning package was an opportunity to model for Ben Barry Agency.

After meeting with Ben Barry in person, I knew that, after a long and successful career in youth work, I was ready to embark on a new adventure and possibly explore a full-time career in modeling. I was ready to have fun and live life to the fullest because we all have only one life to live. My message – Go ahead! Take chances, go where you're not supposed to go, do what you're not supposed to do, and dare to be different if you wish!

. . . .

Unquestionably, my career path has not been without its own hurdles. But my determination to find workable solutions was what helped me succeed. In addition, I have come to appreciate all the resources available to me in everything and in every circumstance. Because knowledge is power, I consider myself an avid knowledge seeker. I read extensively on matters that are of interest to me, especially in areas of finance and wealth management. Equally, I consult with experts in these areas, either paid consultants or by checking in with friends working in these fields. In my career, I have always

184

endeavoured to pursue greater knowledge in order to facilitate my function and effectiveness within my various roles.

My eleven years in management roles definitely exposed me to many learning and development opportunities. Additionally, these roles allowed me to contribute to the development of younger staff, both professionally and individually. For me, it is important to make a difference in the diverse composition of my workplace, and I made use of any opportunity I had to do so.

Using my position to screen and interview many individuals, I hired qualified, capable staff of diverse backgrounds and ethnicities and thus broadened the scope of acceptance within the Ministry for immigrants, minorities, and those with differences. At the very least, I could affect some change within the Ministry at the local level through my dedication and high standards. The atmosphere I left behind when I retired was more relaxed, friendly, and certainly less hostile. The faces of the staff are much more representative of the community we serve. It feels good to know that I have made a difference in the lives of not just the youth I served, but also the staff I worked with and the government agency I worked for.

The Ministry's management pension plan, coupled with my years of exemplary service along with my disciplined financial management, allowed me to take early retirement. It has translated into the gift of time. I spend more time with my wonderful family, especially my beautiful grandbabies. I have more time to pursue my modeling passion and community engagements. Delving into my memory bank of life and career events, I've revisited the emotional roller coaster associated with them, including all the highs and lows of my adventures. This has helped me fulfill the dream of writing this book, my gift to help and encourage others and provide a legacy for my family. I am truly grateful to have my years of hard work and sacrifice pay off and be able to enjoy the rewards and blessings of having given my life to service.

My belief is that if you stare closely and long enough into a rock, you'll begin to see a precious gem and quite possibly a diamond in the rough if you have the right perspective. I say embrace the trying times and create your own possibilities from them!

Chapter 7

CAREER – MANAGEMENT

In October 2003, I was verbally offered one of the two, upper management positions as Deputy Director of Operations (DDO). I accepted instantly without finding out the details of the compensation package the same way I did back when I joined the Correctional Services Division. This time, however, I was not cheated, and my compensation was commensurate with my education, training, and expertise. I officially became a DDO on November 4th, 2003, and I held this title, with a variety of responsibilities, until May 20th, 2015.

In preparation for my new position, I enrolled in the in-service, management training offered by the Ministry through the Alberta Solicitor General and Public Security Training Academy. This was a week-long course designed for all managers with specific topics focused on correctional institution management with a strong emphasis on security and the safety of employees and offenders. Understanding the Canadian Criminal Code's statutes and applications, as well as possessing an exceptional comprehension of the different types of warrants and the legal holding documents as issued by the courts and/or by her representatives was critical management training.

This segment of my training was intensive with periodic updates being necessary throughout my career. As a representative of the Government of Alberta in charge of keeping the community safe while ensuring the rights of the individual offenders were protected, it was incumbent on me as a manager to make sure that a serving offender did not escape lawful custody either through a wrongful release or being at large while on an approved release. Additionally, it was equally mandatory for me to not accept into custody any individual that had not been ordered with valid, legal documents and/or warrants in place to do so.

My preparation for my role as DDO didn't stop there. Other training commenced, including the following courses: Delivering Service Excellence, Performance Management/Legislative Process, Critical Thinking and Project Management, Change Management for Leaders, Employee Labour Relations/Bargaining Unit, and Operational Cost Controls. It was a lot to take in for this next step in my career.

With much excitement and some trepidation, I assumed my new role. I moved from my obscure, private, and relatively quiet unit office (unless when staff or a young person were present) to an open, shared office space at the core of the institution. It was an office I had often referred to as being a "train station" over the years. I felt exposed!

It was a significant change to move into my new office. Male managers had historically occupied this office until Barb came on the scene. Six managers inhabited this space, two each on a rotational, shift schedule using the same desk, phones, and computer. With a perpetual revolving door, every Tom, Dick, and Harry in the building dropped by this office at will. How hygienic could that be? Faced with the reality of my new workspace, my trepidation about the position was replaced with increased panic and anxiety over the state of disarray in which the office was kept.

My unit office had been immaculate because clutter and dirt distracts me. I couldn't and cannot concentrate in clutter. No matter how busy my day would be, I always took ten minutes at the end of it to straighten my desk and empty my trash basket before going home. On Fridays, I cleaned my whole office, including vacuuming, before retiring for the weekend. For me, my workspace must be neat and tidy.

I recall opening my unit office one Monday morning to the smell of bananas, which I dislike with a passion. I searched high and low for the source of the smell but couldn't find it. Unbeknownst to me, a couple of my unit staff, Tony and Mel – who knew that I hated the smell of bananas – had planted banana peels at the very bottom of my paper recycling bin.

Enjoying the joke, they watched me search frantically in vain for the source. Once they realized that I wasn't going to be able work without locating the distraction, one of them offered to help me search and…voilà…the peel was found! By this point, I figured out that they had planted it. Pointing at each other as the guilty party, we all laughed at their successful prank.

I must admit I am what you call a "neat freak". Having things in their proper places is very important to me. I trace this back to my childhood where I was brought up in a large family living in a small space. Living clean and clutter free was our established order of existence. As children, anything we used had to be returned to its rightful place immediately after use. We learnt very quickly that if we wanted to keep anything precious to us, we took care of it. If it was left around unattended, it got destroyed or tossed, end of story! Spending several years in a boarding school and sharing living spaces with many other students in a dormitory also solidified the importance of space and self-care for me. Neat and clean plays a central role in how I operate and work best. Fortunately, with Barb and Bobbi (the other manager hired along with me), we decided to tackle the clutter in the office to the relief of most of the male managers, except for Kyle who happened to be working within this group. Due to his bullying behaviour, this was one of the cons to my new role as I was not thrilled to be in the same workspace with him. (Note: This was years before he was sanctioned and moved to another institution.)

The DDO Managers' group was now composed of three males and three females. This ratio of men to women had never happened before and has never happened since. As a matter of fact, there isn't a single, female, operational manager at the institution as I write this book. The pioneering force of women working towards upper management roles has come to a halt, not because women are incapable or do not aspire to higher, corporate levels (for I will assume that they do) but because they've been unwilling to do so at the cost that we, the pioneering women, paid to get there. In unrelated conversations I've had with a few of the female staff currently at the Centre, they have shared that they feel that the current management structure is not conducive to a balanced life and work existence. They also figure that they have ample time to ascend to the top of their career's corporate ladder if they choose to do so at a later date. Regardless of the reasons behind the lack of women at the corporate helm within the Centre, I *do* know that sacrifice, tenacity, and a strong drive is necessary for achieving higher, corporate levels within any company.

Another thing that detracts women from pursuing higher management is the pay structure. The politics and enormous human responsibilities attached to management positions in the government are often seen as not worthy of the compensation. For instance, institutional and operations managers work twenty-four hour, around-the-clock shifts, including weekends and statutory holidays, without any extra compensation beyond their standard salaries.   On the other hand, unionized supervisors who report to these managers work Monday through Friday with all statutory holidays off. If, for whatever reason, supervisors are required to work outside of regular business hours or on a statutory holiday, they are duly compensated with either overtime pay or banked time in lieu. Therefore, DDO positions are not currently attractive to young, female staff with leadership qualities.

As DDO, I led a team of twenty members, including having the role of direct supervision of a team leader and two unit supervisors. My duties also comprised managing two living units and collaborating with the multiple stakeholders inside and outside of the Centre. I had dealings with the Calgary School Board, Westview Secondary School, religious chaplains, Alberta Health Services (AHS), Psychologists, Psychiatrists, the Calgary Police Service as well as police services and correctional institutions throughout Canada and into some parts of the United States. My responsibilities also extended to special projects, too. I brought one or two with me from my previous position and others were added on. I embraced them all with anticipation, curiosity, and a few hidden fears.   I was unquestionably up for all the challenges of my new role. However, one thing was for certain. I would never again report to Kyle. I may have traded all my comforts and conveniences of my previous office, but I had acquired this one, lone satisfaction with my promotion.

As usual, I worked tirelessly to set myself apart and move my team forward. There had been rumours floating around the building about me before I joined the team. Some of them were founded, for I work extremely hard and had become known for having the same expectations for those around me. People heard that I was a taskmaster who was focused and maintained high expectations for both work ethic and accountability. While these qualities are not bad or undesirable, for some people, the thought of being held accountable for the way they operated was unsettling. Other rumours were unfounded and were basically efforts to discredit this black, immigrant woman who dared to chart her own path by God's grace. Despite the opinions I faced, I was not disturbed. Rather, I embraced the challenge of leading a team with pre-conceived notions and misguided perceptions and, in the end, proving them wrong.

First and foremost, I have always believed in fair and just treatment. Thus, I deliberately applied these same principles to my work life. Secondly, I have always set out to be the kind of leader that I would want to be led by. Therefore, when I became DDO, I set about the journey of building one of the most effective, productive, reputable, and respected teams in the building.

I started by announcing my intention to meet with each team member individually. I requested that they prepare questions ahead of time that they wanted to ask me. Likewise, I would be asking them questions as well. To avoid interruptions, I met with members in the evening towards the end of the late shift when the residents had settled for bed. I started by sharing with them a bit about myself, and then they were given the chance to ask their questions. This interaction gave me the opportunity to affirm and explain (in context) some of the things they'd heard about me as well as dispel some of the myths. Next, I asked questions about each of them: what were their backgrounds, what did they like/not like about their jobs, what could I do to make a situation better, what were their aspirations, and how could I assist them in achieving their goals. I went on to explain to them what my goals were personally and for the team. By the time I had met with a quarter of my team members, word had spread and the tension of a having me as the new manager subsided.

Hence forward, we set up and endeavoured to hold quarterly, team meetings with the goal to hold at least a minimum of two meetings yearly. I turned the dreaded, historically negative, staff meetings into a relaxed, insightful, educative, and collaborative gathering. Also, instead of attempting to bring team members together on their days off for meetings during the week because of our 6 days on, 3 days off shift schedule, I introduced the idea of meeting on a Saturday or Sunday morning before the residents woke up when the whole team was scheduled to work. We held our meetings from 7:00 to 10:00 a.m. where I incorporated team building practices to gear us up. This involved us sharing a home-cooked, hot break-fast/brunch with all the trimmings to start with. Food was contributed by team members as well as by volunteer staff members who arrived at work at 6:00 a.m. to cook for their colleagues in the Centre's industrial kitchen. In this relaxed atmosphere of sharing a meal, we discussed various issues and generated lists of possible solutions. These meetings created a free forum to share concerns and promote creativity. It was an opportunity to set the team's goals and review them often. We also recognized and celebrated team members' personal and professional achievements during these times together. Outside of these meetings, I also initiated and funded monthly, cake cutting ceremonies for team members' birthdays, a practice that lasted for ten years and was emulated by a following manager who had been one of my team members under me. All in all, these meetings became a huge success and a valuable component to our effectiveness.

The staff meetings allowed me to affirm and reinforce my slogan: **If you shine, I shine; If I shine, you shine.** That slogan carried the team for the duration of my time as their manager. It is also my philosophy for service as echoed by one of my former staff members in her letter of endorsement on the following page.

November 7, 2016

RE: Moji Taiwo - Supervisor/Manager - Calgary Young Offender Centre

Ms. Taiwo was my supervisor for a number of years while I was employed at the Calgary Young Offender Centre. She played a big part in helping me through a transition period in my career when I was trying to decide whether I wanted to move forward within corrections or take another career path all together. I saw what she was achieving and the difference she was making for herself and others within corrections and I decided it was a path I wanted to follow. Ms. Taiwo has been a support, mentor and friend for many years, as I have progressed in to a management position within Correctional Services.

Ms. Taiwo was a role model for me at a critical time in my professional development. I learned much from her. She was a great teacher, providing direct and honest feedback. She was always approachable and willing to listen to concerns. She had a positive attitude and strong work ethic that I valued. I respected the dedication and commitment she put into everything she did, always looking for ways to make things better. She was strong and passionate, while being caring and compassionate. She was intelligent with a quick wit and sense of fun. She was a progressive leader.

As my supervisor and as a manager, Ms. Taiwo has been someone I have looked to for advice, she has challenged me to learn and do more and she has always supported me in my endeavors. I appreciate all that I have gained from my experience in working with her.

Sincerely,

Dawn Fraser
Manager
Calgary Youth Attendance Centre
Justice and Solicitor General

The changes to staff meetings weren't the only things I helped improve or facilitate during my tenure as DDO. Other operational enhancements envisioned by me and ultimately adopted by the Centre included the idea of hosting staff training during times of building inactivity, such as weekend mornings and statutory holidays, to capture operational cost savings. In addition, the uninterrupted moments allowed administration leaders to attend the operations meetings as well, thus creating closer contact with frontline members. But my involvement in the betterment of my workplace didn't stop there.

Towards the later part of my employment as DDO with Alberta Justice and Solicitor General in the Correctional Services Division's Young Offender Branch, my focus was dedicated to staff development for young staff and the advocacy for youth within the Centre. My special project portfolio yielded staff training initiatives to better identify and optimize employee skills and strengths. This allowed me to contribute to the research and reconstruction of a new Youth Worker Recruit Training Program. In my facilitator role for this revised program, I participated in the screening, recruitment, and orientation of new employees. As the manager responsible for keeping the Centre's policies and procedures updated, and as the chair of the Youth Advisory Committee, it was my belief that regular, family contact with young people was (and is) crucial to their overall wellbeing. Therefore, I helped augment a policy outlining family visits with young offenders, broadening family visiting hours to cover both days of the weekend instead of families having to choose from either Saturday or Sunday. Similarly working as a proponent for offenders, I assisted in revising the dress code policy for the youth. By introducing uniforms to be issued by the Centre and which were ultimately adopted by the Young Offender Branch, we were thereby able to help prevent incidences of bullying due to situations where offenders wore clothing that ranged from being incredibly worn or tattered to expensive designer clothes. In giving my life to service, I was and have always been on the lookout for areas that I could be of positive influence. Working to improve the lives of both young employees and young offenders was truly satisfying.

. . . .

On the night of March 26th, 2015, I reported for my most dreaded rotation of six graveyard (night) shifts. As a routine – for it was almost a ritual – I settled before my computer to go through my emails and sort the mail in my inbox, identifying reports and memorandums from the previous shifts. I arranged them in priority sequence and began the shift with my cup of coffee in hand, which usually sustained me until about 5:00 a.m.

when my eyes became droopy and my brain turned to mush. By then, I found either a companion on the team to play badminton, table tennis, or pickleball with. In the absence of such a person, I resorted to the exercise room. There, I would put some distance on the treadmill while singing out loud, off-key, and with no apologies about the music playing. These physical activities helped dispel the grogginess of sleep until my replacement showed up at 6:30 a.m.

Before I could get through my routine, a telephone call came in directly to my office, bypassing the Centre's main telephone line. This was highly unusual at that time of the night. Unless the person calling in was a familiar caller that you might expect a call from, not many calls are received during the graveyard shift.

It was Charlotte MacDonald-Allan. She was covering for Barb McKnight, the Centre's Director, who was away on vacation. In itself, Charlotte's call was not alarming to me because she may have just been checking in to see how things were going. However, she asked if I was alone in the office. Receiving a call at midnight and being asked if I was alone? That did *not* sound good!

Charlotte proceeded to inform me that the Young Offender Branch's Executive Director (ED) and a handful of Human Resource personnel would be coming to the Centre in the morning for a meeting with managers, and I would be required to stay over at the end of my night shift. Quite frankly, Charlotte's announcement sounded worse than her initial question, so I inquired further as to what was going on. The upper management group was anticipating budget restraints and restructuring coming up as they usually did every spring, and the spring of 2015 was going to be exceptionally difficult due to the province's economic downturn. Consequently, in collaboration with the Centre's Business Manager, we had generated a few, cost-cutting proposals with regard to operations for the branch in anticipation of the expected, budget cut announcement and were waiting for an invitation to present our yearly proposals. Therefore, the ED's visit with a Human Resource entourage in the absence of our Centre's Director was highly unusual.

The morning finally arrived. The ED and company arrived. With tensions high, the meeting with all the managers began...and the news was even worse than we expected. We were informed that the Centre was going to be closed!

We were paralyzed with astonishment. *No one* had anticipated the closure of an entire facility that served more than half of the province's central to southern region. The consultative, inclusive process for decision-making that we had been familiar with had been totally bypassed. Instead, we faced the shocking consequences of a unilateral decision coming straight from the head office in Edmonton.

All our preparations for budget cuts and the proposals generated ahead of time had been futile. The same executive team, who had formerly encouraged, inspired, and motivated us to be innovative, had failed to consult with us to brainstorm creative solutions before reaching such a life-altering decision. Instead, they had taken it upon themselves to decide for the hundreds of staff and young people in the Centre with no consideration given to the negative effects this move would make.

Furthermore, this decision violated the core values of the government – respect, accountability, integrity, and excellence. Respect and integrity were sure lacking. Personally, I was in support of cost-cutting measures. However, I totally disagreed with the way the government had decided these so-called "savings" were to be achieved.

Because of the shutdown, many offenders affected would be moved to Edmonton. Others would have to be transported between the two cities and from other smaller locations for any court appearances. As a supposed, cost saving action, that decision didn't make any sense to me. Furthermore, transporting that many youth during the winter months on snow- and ice-covered, Alberta highways also raised safety concerns for me. To top it off, families from southern Alberta would have to travel all the way to Edmonton to see their children. Youth who relied on volunteer visitors because they

202

didn't have a family or the family could not afford transportation costs would be out of luck, and they'd have to do without visitors. Access to legal guardians and other community support services would be conducted by phone instead of in person. Most of these adolescents had a hard enough time comprehending the system and processing their issues when dealing face-to-face with their service providers, but now they would have to complete these same services over the telephone within limited time frames? I absolutely could not see the value in these measures, especially with regard to what it would cost the young people.

One by one, all of us managers met with HR personnel who presented us with envelopes containing our departure offers. We were instructed not to discuss our offers with anyone at that time because the department still needed us to present a unified front when breaking the news to our other team members. Throughout the day, we met with staff currently on duty, called in members scheduled for afternoon shifts to report for duty early, and employees that had worked the night before were woken up to report to the Centre as soon as possible. The depressing task of informing the rest of the staff was set in motion.

With the use of social media amongst staff, news travelled fast. Soon, the entire Centre was flooded with calls from staff on days off, out of the city, other institutions, and community partners. Several people were terminated, others were offered redeployment (but to where?), and some were simply given an empty envelope with no offer or severance. However, for those of us presented with a choice in our envelopes, we had to make our decision regarding our offers within forty-five days. Employees without offers were left completely in limbo. The Centre itself was slated to close in ninety days and be rebranded as a holding facility. The entire process was poorly orchestrated without much forethought at all. The staff had questions that the HR representatives could not answer. It was a very sad day!

By the time all the Centre's employees were notified of the impending closure, their loss of employment or redeployment, and I had an opportunity to open and review the contents of the envelope presented to me, I had been at work for almost twenty-four hours. I was ready to collapse. Heading home, I essentially crashed from lack of sleep and emotional exhaustion. I was totally drained!

As the most senior member of the operational management team, I was given two scenarios to choose from. Choice one: Remain with the organization under what I considered absurd and unfair working conditions under the new, reorganized structure. This would consist of permanent afternoon and night shifts without shift work compensation. Choice two: Accept a pre-determined, non-negotiable severance package as indicated in the letter. To say that I was tired and disappointed at the process after thirty plus years of dedicated service was an understatement. I was deeply upset that the terms of my employment were being redrawn arbitrarily and dictated to me. I had always been the architect of my own destiny up to that point. If I accepted the offer to continue working under the new conditions set out for me, I would not be home with my husband in the evenings and on most nights, meaning that we'd both be going in opposite directions. After all that we had sacrificed and worked towards over the years, that arrangement was not acceptable to me. On the other hand, if I accepted the severance payment, I would be retiring two years earlier than my planned retirement date. My mind was in a quandary.

The following two weeks took me on a roller coaster ride of emotions. I proceeded to closely examine my professional, social, and financial status in order to make my decision. I have always been a planner. Always. This has aided me in reaching final decisions with confidence even in the face of uncertainty and challenges. Nevertheless, I was still rattled by the suddenness of the decision forced upon me. I had to thoroughly sort out my feelings of betrayal at the hands of the head honchos in Edmonton, the possibility of facing the sudden and unexpected and abrupt departure from my professional atmosphere and its social connections, and of course, I needed to figure out my family's finances. I decided to take one week off work to sit down and map out both scenarios.

After all that had gone on since the announcement, including self-reflection, I was leaning towards taking early retirement. The next step would be convincing my husband that it was the best decision for me and for us. That would take some effort, thus the importance of taking the time off to map out what our future would look like if I took this big step.

To be perfectly honest, by 2013, I had been growing restless with what I was doing and had begun to explore other, more challenging, employment opportunities within and outside of the department. I was even open to exploring short-term, exchange placements at other institutions or in the community. It was during this time that I had begun to seriously pay attention to my retirement plan by calculating my family's assets and liabilities along with a future career change.

I had qualified to receive unreduced, pension payments two years earlier but had felt at that point that I was too young to retire, and hence, my quest for a possible, career change. This innocent plan of mine from two years earlier to map out my retirement proved to be the catalyst that tilted my ultimate decision towards early retirement. Since I already knew that my full pension would not be jeopardized, it appeared to be the best choice.

During my week off to contemplate this major, life decision, I used all the resources I had available to me. As mentioned earlier, I believe that knowledge is power, and I have a knack for acquiring from, sharing with, and learning from other people. I started by consulting with my pension plan's board for current pension payment information based on various retirement dates. Then, my husband and I consulted with our financial adviser(s) to obtain a complete picture of our current holdings, future investments (from my severance payment), and investment returns in relation to our living expenses. Lastly, we consulted with our accountant to review our taxes for the year considering the severance I was being offered and the various ways in which to maximize our tax plan. The process proved to be more beneficial than expected. As eloquently stated by that Scotiabank commercial, we found out that we were "richer than we thought".

With our financial plans taken care off, I faced head-on my feelings of betrayal and those that accompanied my professional departure from the career that I loved. I did so mainly by seizing the opportunity to itemize all the things on my bucket list of things I still wanted to do or accomplish. This included spending more time with my grandbabies and travelling whenever I wanted to. In retirement, I would not have to trade shifts with other managers in order to take time off anymore. What a freeing feeling!

So, I made my decision. I would leave the Ministry of Alberta Justice and Solicitor General and retire. Other employees, mainly those of us who qualified for unreduced, pension payments, also retired. Many of the staff accepted the severance packages offered and went searching for other jobs, taking with them all the capital and training manpower we had invested into them as part of the management team's succession planning.

Between the time I reached my decision to leave and my last day on May 20th, 2015, the Centre was like a ghost town. People walked around like zombies wearing mournful faces. I felt content to have had a choice, but I felt incredibly sad for others less fortunate in what ended up being a messy affair.

Many employees were left looking for answers, but none were provided. Not content to wallow in their sorrow, the unionized members of the Centre organized themselves. With the support of community stakeholders, they protested and rallied in front of the provincial government building in downtown Calgary until their voices were heard.

The provincial election was held a few weeks into the protest, and a new government was elected. Guess what? The decision to close the Calgary Young Offender Centre was halted, and decisions were reversed. It was good news for the young people in custody, their families and guardians, and for the staff whose lives were being destabilized. But for some, it was already too late. They had accepted their severance pay and moved on, and others, like me, retired to a future with new adventures.

The whole fiasco resulted in the regrettable loss of many highly trained and experienced workers, not to mention the money paid out in severance. The CYOC's staff will have to be rebuilt, a task that will cost even more money, time, and training. I believe all of this could have been avoided if the head honchos had consulted us – the management team – to review our proposals and constructively negotiate the future of the Centre. Meaningful, problem-solving conversations could have addressed necessary, yet reasonable, cost-cutting measures to respond wisely to the economic downturn yet preserve the integrity of the service we provided and the investment already built into CYOC and its team members. The way they went about it was completely dishonest and detrimental to those affected.

With the reversal of the closure, I actually received an offer to have my job back...to which I resoundingly replied, "No thanks!" My job was done. It was time for new challenges, time for new territory to be conquered, time for new adventures to be embarked upon.

The following excerpt, written in my retirement card by one of the staff, summed it up for me...

"Three things come to mind when I think of Moji Taiwo: Achievement, Relationships, and Thinking.

"Under achievement, I think of two things. I would describe Moji as someone who drives for results. She understands what outcomes are important and maximizes resources to achieve results aligned with the goals of the organization.

"Secondly under achievement, I think of her agility. This is best described as her ability to anticipate, assess, and readily adapt to changing priorities, maintain resilience in times of uncertainty, and effectively work in a changing environment.

"Regarding relationships, Moji Taiwo builds collaborative environments. She leads and contributes to the conditions and environments that allow people to work collaboratively and productively. She also develops networks, connecting and building trust in relationships with different stakeholders.

"Finally, I would describe Moji Taiwo as a systems thinker, someone who keeps broader impacts and connections in mind. One of her strongest attributes is creative problem solving. [She's] a leader who can assess options and implications in new ways to achieve solutions."
Brent Keller, Programs Supervisor, CYOC

Immediately after my retirement, I planned a summer road trip, and we ended up with two trips. My husband and I, along with another couple who are close friends, went on a road trip through the southwestern part of the province of Alberta. Then, my husband and I took another trip through the Rocky Mountains down to the west coast of British Columbia with our destination being Vancouver. It was a wonderful opportunity to explore and enjoy this great country. I was off to a great start in my retirement!

Chapter 8
GIVING WITH GRACE, RECEIVING WITH GRATITUDE

While I am not particularly religious, I was raised in a Moslem home, educated in both Catholic and Methodist schools, and was surrounded by extended family members who practiced both Islam and Christianity. Thus, I grew up with a deep spirituality rooted in connectivity with all living species, and I developed a spirituality based on demonstrated love for all God's creation and a spirituality based on fearlessness to be my unique self, to speak the truth, and to manifest the purpose of my creation here on earth. Spirituality is not only something that I believe in, it is who and what I live for. Out of my spirituality, I have discovered how to give with grace and receive with gratitude.

Family

When our family left Lethbridge and returned to Calgary in August of 1984 to assume my new position at the Strathmore Youth Development Centre, we were beginning another

213

important chapter in our lives. After the completion of my training and receiving my permanency letter for employment, it was time to settle the family.

First, we rented a modest, two-bedroom apartment in the southeast part of the city for quicker access to the TransCanada Highway for my commute to Strathmore. Then, our first daughter, Lolade, was registered in school for kindergarten while we simultaneously searched for reputable childcare services for after school care and for our younger daughter, Adejoke.

By the summer of 1985, after my husband returned from a trip to our birth country of Nigeria, it was becoming more likely that our long-term home would be Canada. Up until that point, we had been of the mind that we would eventually return to Nigeria. However, the employment prospects and our expectations for life in Nigeria were less than ideal. Therefore, we decided to remain in Canada for a few more years while conditions hopefully improved in Nigeria.

With this decision made, my attention turned to my children's education. I had been volunteering in Lolade's kindergarten classes and had noticed how quiet, immigrant, and visible minority students were relegated to the back of the classroom while more boisterous, white students – mostly boys – got the bulk of the teacher's attention. Then, my daughter brought home her first report card, which was not favourable at all. I reviewed her report card, which stated that she couldn't recite her alphabet or count her numbers. I knew this was not at all correct because this child had spent her preschool years with me at the University of Lethbridge's library, was exposed to early learning opportunities, and was encouraged and taught with regard to the basics of preschool readiness. In fact, she was ahead of her age group, especially in reading. When I questioned her as to who had administered the test, she replied that it was the "student teacher"...but it had been the homeroom teacher who had completed the report card. I knew then and there that I had to become more involved in my children's education.

I started to volunteer as a classroom assistant on a weekly basis at the school. I volunteered at special events such as field trips, cultural days, and Christmas pageants. Next, I very specifically made a point of meeting all the teachers at the onset of a new school year to discuss my children and their education. In those meetings, I established an understanding of behavioural and educational expectations that I desired to see from the schools and from my children before the first report card was ever sent home. The results were phenomenal. The teachers felt supported, and my children, usually being a part of only a few black children in the school community, felt comfortable and focused on their learning. I also became popular with their friends. I continued to meet with the teachers and volunteer until my oldest daughter got to grade twelve and informed me that I didn't have to come to her school anymore.

Community Involvement

My experience with the challenges immigrant children face in education became a motivating factor for me to form a women's support group for immigrants. While we waited to decide when (or if) we were going to return to Nigeria, I was determined to make something of myself, not just for myself and my family, but for my community as well. I desired to expand my service.

First of all, I decided that a women's group was needed – a group to provide immigrants with opportunities to get together from time to time for social activities, common support, and provide an environment for our second-generation, Canadian-born children to play with and learn from others that looked like them. In 1985, there were not many black kids in Calgary schools, especially with unique, African names, and the few such students in attendance were hardly acknowledged by the teachers. When they got attention in class, it was not always positive. As immigrant, black women, we needed each other for mutual support, and through our organization, provide support to our children to combat the marginalization being perpetrated

216

on them in schools. I shared my idea of forming such a group with a few sister friends, and they saw value in the plan. As a result of that encouragement, the Nigerian Women's Association of Calgary (NWAC) was formed in 1986.

Sister friends of Nigerian heritage and through marriage formed the core of NWAC, such as the late Mona Okafor (RIP), Adenike Olagundoye, Grace Oyelusi, Bernie Gbalajobi, Emily Daramola, Agnes Ibelo, Esther Metuh, Josephine Orgor, and Florence Adereti. Naturally, I was the Public Relations Officer (PRO) for our group given my background in Radio Arts, accompanied by my comfort and ability with public speaking and my modeling hobbies that thrust me into the public eye. Being as I had taken some classes on runway walks, poses, and makeup artistry by then, I eagerly shared my knowledge with our volunteer models in preparation for our fundraising shows for NWAC. I hosted all the association's events from birthday parties to our annual gala events and fashion shows. I was also the backstage handler for our cultural, group dancers who performed at Heritage Days and at the Olympic Plaza during the 1988 Calgary Winter Olympics. We had so much fun and received huge recognition from the City of Calgary and other ethnic communities. Unfortunately, NWAC dissolved in 1990 due to differences of opinion between a few members of the association regarding direction.

With the termination of NWAC, I found more time to pursue other volunteer opportunities where my passion and skills aligned to benefit the community. I joined the YMCA of Calgary's Minority Achievement Program as a member of the Steering Committee for the Minority Youth Program from 1990 to 1994. In conjunction with my committee involvement, I also facilitated life skills and coaching support to immigrant young people who were attempting to adapt to their new schools and home country. Young, immigrant parents had their own adjustment issues and did not always understand the challenges their children were faced with. I became a sounding board for them. Due to the nature of my job as a youth worker, I could understand what they were going through and provide them with different coping skills. During this period, I was also involved with the Congress of Black Women, Calgary Chapter, promoting education in diversity and cultural awareness through classroom presentations and participation in yearly, African Heritage Month celebrations. I was recognized with certificates and appreciation plaques for both services.

By 1993, it was clear to my husband and I that Canada was to be our permanent home. Thus, we needed to focus more on establishing our Nigerian roots here for our children. Hold on to that thought! It was then that the Nigerian community in Calgary unexpectedly lost one of her own and a respected community member. This quickly cemented our commitment to

218

create a constructive group for Nigerians where their children could grow, thrive, and be supported.

From this unfortunate incident, and as small as our population was in the city, a group of us brother and sister friends decided to form the Nigerian Canadian Association of Calgary (NCAC) in 1994. My husband and I were founding members, and I served as an executive member for ten consecutive years. During my tenure, I held positions as Public Relations Officer, Humanitarian Officer, Social Events Coordinator, Vice President, and President. I am so proud of the Association – its growth, achievements, and contributions to the cultural mosaic of the country – and its prominence in the City of Calgary.

NCAC is a non-profit, non-political organization with its centre of activities and headquarters based in the northeast of Calgary, Alberta, Canada. Since inception, NCAC holds free, annual summer picnics and Christmas (year end) parties for all. These events are open to everyone and have been attended by hundreds of people in the community with no restrictions. Nigerians love to celebrate through the sharing of both cultural and western food, through music with live DJs, and through sports activities, games, crafts, and face painting for the children. In 2015, the Association added Stampede breakfasts to their schedule of events to honour our community of Calgary and join in the celebration of the historic, world-renowned Calgary

Stampede. In 2016, NCAC entered a dance group that participated in the festivities of the Calgary Stampede Parade. Then in 2017, NCAC unveiled its first ever float at the Parade. It is with great pleasure that NCAC contributes to fellow Nigerians and the broader Calgarian and Canadian community through its involvement in many events.

In commemoration of Nigeria's Independence from Great Britain on October 1, 1960, NCAC celebrates a special, annual, gala event that is held on the first Saturday in October. The NCAC Gala, as it has come to be known, showcases Nigerian culture, food, fashion, and the artistic and academic talents of our children along with celebrating volunteerism and community involvement. From a humble party in 1994, the current Gala hosts, on average, seven hundred guests, including community and political dignitaries. We have hosted and danced with the Mayor(s) of Calgary, the Chief(s) of Police and or designate(s), representatives from both the provincial and federal governments, the CEO(s) and representatives of major oil and gas companies in Calgary, and many more supporters.

The purpose of the NCAC Gala is to be a source of fundraising for the Association's special programs, which includes bursaries for our children who consistently earn top-notch grades from grades 7 to post-secondary levels. It supports life skills programs for preteens and teens and mentorship programs for post-secondary students. The funding from this event also goes towards the operating costs of the volunteer executives and the maintenance of the Nigerian Canadian Association of Calgary's Community House.

In 1999, through the Association's fundraising efforts, the membership raised enough funds with matching grants from the Alberta Gaming and Liquor Commission to make a cash purchase of its current headquarters. It was a great achievement to purchase a property without a bank loan and a blessing to be a part of this great establishment in my community! Now, in its 23rd year since formation, NCAC is thriving with a much larger membership population filled with capable, innovative, and progressive young leaders.

NCAC's mission and objectives as stated in its bylaw:

• *To exhibit and promote, in a discrete, inclusive, peaceful and unobtrusive manner, those aspects of Nigerian culture and heritage that would contribute positively to the Canadian cultural mosaic.*

• *To encourage a positive environment where members of the Association can get together from time to time for social and multicultural engagement, dialogue and interaction.*

• *To provide a cultural connection and identity, as needed, for children of Nigerian parentage and any other person who desires to identify with the Association's objectives, as more particularly outlined in the Bylaw.*

221

• To create a network, and if necessary a platform, for rendering reasonable and lawful assistance, as deemed fit by the Association, to members who may require support from time to time, and to Nigerians arriving newly to Calgary to facilitate their transition into the larger Calgary community.

• To act as the focal point of a network that would promote social and economic benefit of its members and society in general.

As with the YMCA's Minority Achievement Program, I created and facilitated Life Skills classes for our NCAC youth from ages twelve to seventeen, a class that was held every Sunday throughout the school season from 1994 to 2005 with a revival in 2015. Topics such as self-esteem building, peer pressure, making choices, the importance of education, and many others were covered. Other women in the Association also introduced and taught our children Nigerian culture through music and dance performances.

"Being the child of members of the Calgary Nigerian-Canadian Association (sic), I really had no choice as to whether I wanted to take the community-offered, Life Skills course. At that time in my life, I probably would have rather been playing videos games or sports with my

friends. Now looking back, I understand the importance of the course and how it has helped me progress in my career. The course gave me the tools to adequately evaluate my beliefs, consider career choices, and generally understand the role I played in my community and the larger society. The course instructor was also great and quite knowledgeable with the materials. She is someone who understands and can integrate the homeland and Canadian culture. To this day, I see her more as a mentor than just a friend of the family."

Trevor – Accountant, Course Year: 1998

"I attended a Life [Skills] course with Moji Taiwo when I was around 13 years old. It was great being in an environment with my peers sharing our experiences and the challenges of being adolescent, female, first-generation Canadians. Moji was patient, and she listened. She was fun and gave us great ideas and guidance. She created a safe space for us girls to share and bond. After 20 years, I am still a very close friend with many of the other ladies that participated in that."

Lynn – Energy Analyst, Year: 1995

"I was fortunate to participate in Life Skills classes at an early age (tweens). The exact year eludes me, but it is safe

to say the time frame is greater than twenty years [ago]. The most enjoyable aspect of the class was coming together with other girls my age and building friendships and developing camaraderie."

Lola – BScN, M.H.A, RN – Charge Nurse

"I participated in Moji Taiwo's Life Skills program during the period of 1994-1996 and attribute her program in helping me become the confident, successful woman I am today. Moji's program not only gave the young girls and boys of my generation a safe place where we could hang out and socialize with our peers, but [it gave us] an opportunity to explore and deal effectively with the demands and challenges of being young adolescents. The program content was very informative and explored areas such as the development stages of adolescence, peer pressure, building and maintaining healthy and positive relationships, health and wellness, and money management. I highly recommend Moji's program for today's youth who may be facing their own set of challenges as young adults. Moji's program will not only assist you in building the necessary skills and foundation to survive adolescence, but [will provide] an opportunity to

develop your potential to succeed in life. Thank you, Moji, for giving us the tools to become successful young adults and for giving us a head start in life."

Cynthia – M.S.W., RSW – Community Social Worker

"I participated in the Life Skills course offered through the Nigerian Canadian Association of Calgary during my early preteen years. I really appreciated the fact that Moji provided a platform for us youth to bond and have a safe space to discuss issues that may have been difficult to discuss at home. The program was both engaging and interactive, and Moji was very knowledgeable about the material she presented to us. Moji has a genuine passion for helping youth reach their maximum potential. She has not only proven to be an inspiration to the youth in the Nigerian Canadian community, but [she's] also a mentor to those of us entering our careers."

Amanda – B.A. – Youth Counselor

"I first met with Moji as a newcomer to Calgary, and I was having a problem with one of my kids. Moji helped me with tips on how to parent my kid. I think with the experience that Moji has, there is no doubt this is a good program that every family (especially newcomers to this country) should access. Moji not only helped the family

225

settle in Calgary, but [she] also was an encouragement to this writer who went back to school, earned my MSW, and now is a social worker in Calgary."
Anonymous

In 2010, I was awarded the "Community Leadership Award" by NCAC for my contributions as a founding member, leader, volunteer, and an avid supporter of the Association. I was recognized again in 2015 for continued leadership and community service within my beloved Association.

As the population of Nigerians in Calgary grew, so was the diverse, tribal composition of the community resulting in the formation of many, smaller sub-groups (affiliates of NCAC). Nigeria, per the 2015 census, is classified as the seventh most populated country in the world with approximately 188 million people, approximately five hundred ethnic groups, and five hundred spoken dialects. English is the official language of the country complemented by three, major native languages – Hausa, Ibo, and Yoruba. My heritage is of the Yoruba ethnic group, and I was born and raised in Lagos. Lagos, a metropolitan city of approximately twenty million people, is a city where anyone is everyone, being a melting pot of cultures, languages, religion, economies, and social mingling and intermingling. Growing up in the city as a Nigerian, not much relevance was placed on my ethnicity or the dialect I spoke. I was simply a member of a larger community of many ethnicities living together.

Recently, the formation of ethnic sub-groups in Calgary has strengthened the base of NCAC as a community group. However, it wasn't always so. When the first sub-group was formed, the Igbo Cultural Association of Calgary (ICAC), it caused division amongst our once peaceful community. Early in its formation, some of its individuals introduced divisive, ethnic beliefs from Nigeria that served to highjack the NCAC operations. They did so by manipulating member numbers in their favour for their own personal gain and through unscrupulous activities conducted at NCAC headquarters. True community was threatened.

Now, I have always been a strong advocate of cohesion, unity, and bringing people together in harmony regardless of differences. Thus, a few of us founding members of NCAC appealed to some of our NCAC co-founders, now ICAC members, to ask them to reason with their ethnic brothers. However, our efforts failed to see peace materialize. Unwilling to stand by and watch our beloved community association that we had worked so hard to establish be destroyed by these troublemakers, we decided to confront the aggressors at their own level, hence the formation of the Yoruba Foundation Calgary.

I, along with a few brother friends who shared my Yoruba ethnicity – Wale Gbalojobi, Wale Onabadejo, Dr. Sam Afolayan, and Supo Lawal – gathered in my kitchen in 2004 to brainstorm how to preserve our beloved NCAC. We needed to generate numbers to counter this attack on unity. Additionally, we realized that those of us of non-Ibo heritage needed a supportive group that could strategize on how to thwart the aggression from these few people who wished to use ethnicity and differences to bring division. The only way to create this collective base was to form the Yoruba Foundation Calgary (YFC). Because of our efforts, NCAC was rescued from a group of people that did not care about our wellbeing or our reputation as Nigerians in the City of Calgary.

Since its formation, YFC has proven to be a huge support base for NCAC culturally and in leadership. Working in harmony with NCAC, it has provided additional support to Nigerians of Yoruba descent inside and outside of Calgary and providing their children with extra support and avenues to network. In 2014, the YFC celebrated its tenth anniversary in grand style, hosting approximately 500 guests.

Mission Statement:

The Yoruba Foundation Calgary (YFC) is a Nigerian-Canadian, ethno–cultural association that embraces all Canadians and lovers of the Yoruba heritage, culture, and tradition regardless of race, gender, age, economic status, religious or political affiliations. Our sole objective is to advance Yoruba culture and heritage in Calgary. As part of this objective, the YFC is committed to developing family enrichment programs.

The Yoruba foundation encourages the interchange of ideas among Nigerians and continues to cooperate with other Nigerian, ethnic organizations in Canada.

Our value system is rooted in the principles of multiculturalism, the fundamental principles upon which the Canadian society was built and continues to exist and function.

During a program planning session for YFC in 2013, an idea to host a Mother's Day luncheon was suggested by a community sister friend, Yinka Oladele. Yinka consulted with me and another sister friend, staunch community leader – Nike Olagundoye, on whether the program was needed and feasible. We all agreed that it was a great idea. Therefore, a plan for the event was put into motion, and the first Mother's Day luncheon was held (which I missed due to a prior commitment to fun times in Vegas, if you know what I mean). The event received rave reviews by the attendees.

In 2014, the three of us decided to expand the luncheon to a conference and not limit the guest list to only Yoruba women.

Instead, we extended the invitation to all women from all walks of life, 18 years of age and upward. We decided to name our Mother's Day gathering Women of Vision (WOV). We've made the conference a forum for education, camaraderie, networking, empowerment, inspiration, and an avenue for younger women to learn from experienced women and vice versa. We've invited strong, positive, professional women (and men) as guest speakers who are subject matter experts on topics such as Money Management and Finance, Business and Entrepreneurship, Health and Wellness (emotional, mental, & physical), Parenting Skills, Building/Strengthening Relationships, and Breast Care. Of course, we're not all about just business with no fun, for fun is my middle name! We have also incorporated food, music, and Zumba (an exercise dance) as standards at the WOV conference, which is held annually between late April to early May. We believe that the women who participate and attend the event own it, and therefore, at the end of each conference, women are encouraged to submit topic ideas for the following year. The event topic is then drawn from the entries.

It is sometimes ironic how life comes full circle. I started my community advocacy through the formation of the Nigerian Women's Association of Calgary in 1987, and here I am in 2016, once again a member of a group championing women's causes. I am truly grateful for all the opportunities I've had to pursue my passion of enriching lives along my life's path. My mission and purpose has always been to touch as many lives as I can, leaving traces of kindness, generosity, and everlasting happiness behind. As such, I have not limited my influence and involvement to just my immediate, ethnic community, but I've extended my commitments and contributions in society well beyond my Nigerian culture. My life is so fulfilled!

Over the years, I have been honoured to be involved with and contribute to many initiatives promoting a safe, inclusive, and diverse society. One such focus was through the United Nation's Multimedia and Multiculturalism Initiative – a panel discussion on how ethnicity affects the media in Calgary. I have participated in the Calgary Police Services (CPS) Diversity Conferences, delivering educational and information sessions to CPS recruit classes on cultural awareness, understanding, and sensitivity. Currently, I sit as a board member on the Chief's African Communities Advisory Board for CPS. This position allows me to act as a liaison between African communities and the city police by making recommendations on potential avenues to build trust within the African communities in Calgary, thereby attracting more visible minority members to the service. I equally serve as a resource for CPS and its programs and services, relaying the opportunities available to the young people within the local African communities.

As a mother, a professional, and an advocate for family cohesion, I sat as a member of the Board of Directors for the Parent Support Association of Calgary for many years. The Parent Support Association is a volunteer-driven, not-for-profit organization that integrates professional training and education with parent-led, support groups. It's an organization that provides programs and support for parents experiencing struggles with their teenage children as well as family members of any age who suffer from Fetal Alcohol Spectrum Disorder (FASD).

Giving Back

I haven't limited myself to just community involvement and advocacy. I also participate in meaningful causes close to my heart such as Betty's Walk for ALS (Lou Gehrig disease), a disease that causes the death of neurons that control voluntary muscle movements. I became aware of this terrible disease when one of my life mentors, whom I came to know through his volunteer service at my work, was diagnosed with it.

Mr. Bill Pratt was a prominent figure and businessman in Calgary. He designed and built Heritage Park in Calgary and was the President and COO of the 1988 Calgary Winter Olympics. He volunteered to work with one of our most difficult young men in the Centre at the time. This particular teen was due to be released into the community, but his home environment was not conducive to his future success. The family was heavily involved in criminal activities, but Mr. Pratt wanted to make a difference, for he loved challenges. He took this boy under his wing, provided him with training on his ranch, and connected him with people in industry. That troubled boy turned his life around as a result and became a successful adult. He was also one of Bill Pratt's last projects. As ALS attacks the muscles rapidly, within a few months, the jovial, boisterous, rugged, kind-hearted cowboy was left without mobility. Ramona Deer, my husband, and I visited with him at his ranch in Cochrane, Alberta, when he could still speak, but his voice was also taken soon after. Bill Pratt passed away in 1999. I was extremely blessed to have met and been a friend of this very humble man. When I walk the Betty's Walk for ALS, I walk for Mr. Bill Pratt!

As a person who believes in complete wellness and wellbeing and "living life" to the utmost heights, I take nothing for granted. As part of my overall interest in this area, I desire to promote wellness and research for future generations, particularly for those of African descent, and as a legacy of medical history for my children and grandchildren especially. Therefore, I chose to participate in the Canadian Longitudinal Study on Aging (CLSA) in 2014.

CLSA is a large, national, long-term study of more than 50,000 men and women who are between the ages of 45 and 85 when recruited. The participants are followed until 2033 or their death. The aim of the CLSA is to find ways to help us live long and live well, as well as to understand why some people age in a healthy fashion while others do not.

The research study's data collection is completed every two years with a combination of oral questions, plus a complete physical, medical, emotional/psychological analysis. A report of any abnormality in the testing is provided to me as a participant to be shared with my family physician for follow-up. By participating in the study, I feel that I've been given a gift of extraordinary health care. Any irregularity in my tests allows for preemptive care rather than reactive treatments. It is good to give!

In addition, as a recipient of blood donations in 1983 after losing such a substantial amount of blood when delivering my second daughter, I have always felt that I must give back to others in some health-related way. While I can't give blood because of where I was born and previous exposure to tuberculosis, I decided to sign my driver's license for organ donation. It's the least I could do for the gift of life I received through my blood transfusion.

Another cause that I continue to devote my time to is the annual, door-to-door canvassing for the Canadian Diabetes Association because diabetes runs in my family. Diabetes is a chronic, often debilitating disease that is sometimes fatal. For those with this disease, their bodies either cannot produce insulin or cannot use the insulin it produces properly. Insulin is an important hormone that controls the amount of glucose (sugar) in the blood and is needed to process that glucose as an energy source for the body. Thus, diabetes leads to high blood sugar levels, which can, in turn, damage organs, blood vessels, and nerves. While this awful disease can afflict anybody, it is said to be very common among Black and Hispanic people. All donations collected through door-to-door canvassing and other means are used to conduct research and provide education, treatment options, and support for individuals and the diabetic community.

I'm sure you remember our bad experience with that landlady in Lethbridge. Not only did that incident inspire my husband and I to purchase our own home, we also started a rental property, holdings company to provide housing while being kind and compassionate landlords. This way of thought led to another way of paying it forward in acknowledgment of the people who came to our assistance in our time of need, particularly in the area of housing. Hence, my husband and I decided to host international students in our principal home.

Hosting foreign students exposed our children to other cultures. It taught them how to share their spaces and relate to different people. It gave them opportunities to see the world through other people's views. For over ten years, we housed, fed, nurtured, educated, learnt from, and shared cultures with many students. As a result, we have created some long-lasting friendships with individuals from various parts of the world and Canada (Quebec City). The students' ages ranged from 12 years old all the way to 40 years old, and they arrived from Japan, China, Singapore, Mexico, Brazil, Switzerland, Taiwan, Australia, South Korea, Saudi Arabia, Tunisia, and Indonesia. We still maintain contact with several of them through social media and receive updates on their lives, careers, and families. Some send Christmas cards while others have made Calgary home upon the completion of their education. Nancy (from Indonesia) is a professional accountant and a homeowner in Calgary. We are so proud of her! Many of the souvenirs from the different countries and pictures of the students remain prominently displayed on our mantle to this day. The experience and feeling of sharing has been rewarding for our whole family.

The Importance of Networks

Having a network of resourceful people is very important in one's life, even more important than money. In addition, it is especially essential in the lives of immigrants who must start building their lives in a new country from scratch while fostering the future success of their children. There is a life-long worth and value in creating and maintaining a network of individuals that can help you attain the goals you have for yourself and for your family and who you, in turn, can help as well when those opportunities arise. This network can include anyone from family, friends, acquaintances, co-workers, experts and professionals, teachers and mentors, successful and positive people, and like-minded people with similar goals. Each plays a role in furthering your success.

Bill Pratt was one of the many great people in my own, personal network. Through Mr. Pratt, my oldest daughter, who had just completed her first year of university, secured her first, significant, summer job as a pari-mutuel (taking wagers on horse races – yeah, I didn't know what it was either) at the Stampede Grounds. This is just one of the many ways this man blessed my family and me.

Other friends and connections played important roles in my network. Benwar and Makda, friends from Eritrea who operated a Superstore gas station within walking distance from our home, hired all three of our children in different stages of their education. Getting to know them as friends opened the door for them to know our family, which, in turn, led to these work opportunities for our kids.

I must mention Jennifer Foster, whom I met at Elsie's Hair Studio while getting my hair done. Jennifer was (is) a manager with Alberta Health Services (AHS). When I shared with her that my daughter, Lolade, was a second-year, nursing student and needed exposure to the field as she continued her studies, Jennifer met with her and subsequently gave her a summer placement opportunity as a unit clerk on her unit. Being hardworking and disciplined, Lolade did not disappoint. In fact, she remained on the unit and eventually moved up as an "undergraduate nurse" and then as a registered nurse. Since then, she has moved around and within the hospital system, and she is now a charge nurse. Jennifer cracked the door open for my daughter to gain extra experience in her field of study that led to advancements in her career. I am extremely appreciative of her efforts on Loly's behalf.

Then, there was Tony Kakpovbia, a pipeline-corrosion, engineering specialist who ran a testing lab. I met Tony at NCAC, and he and his family became very close to ours and still are to this day. He hired Lolade the same summer she worked as a pari-mutuel. She was such a trooper! That girl worked two (and eventually three) summer jobs at one time.

To tell you the truth, all my children worked more than one job during school breaks. My daughter, Adejoke, worked at Benwar and Makda's gas station while she held down a job with the Young Canadians (of the Calgary Stampede) as a costumer. Remember, she is the daughter who is now in the fashion world as a designer. Also, while working at the same gas station on weekends, my son, a Computer Information Technology System student, was acquiring valuable work experience from

"Wmode", a mobile phone testing company owned by Dennis Woronuk. Dennis was a neighbour and the father of Adedeji's good friend, Mike. Mike spent a lot of time at my house back in those days, and this connection led to his second job. My kids' tenacity and strong work ethic was the foundation to their ability to hold down multiple jobs at a time in order to meet their goals in life.

There is another important point that I am making here through these stories, and that is that "we reap what we sow" in life. No goodness goes unrewarded, and we just never know where that reward will come from. I believe that the connections we make in life have purpose. Therefore, as we make friends, meet up with people in our everyday world, extend our service and kindness as we journey in life – that is, develop our networks – we create the opportunity for open doors and the rewards of those connections somewhere in the future.

Sharing Knowledge

Sharing our knowledge is part of how we can give to and bless others. Professionally, my passion for sharing my knowledge has extended to guest speaking engagements, mentorship, and board memberships. I have taken on these roles as my honour and privilege.

I have played an active role in piquing the interest of many new students to explore career options in policing, youth care, corrections, and the justice system. From 2009 to 2015, I served as a member of Lethbridge College's School of Justice Studies and on the Advisory Committee for Bow Valley College's Youth and Justice Studies. I had the privilege of speaking to students annually during their program orientation. I also lent my expertise in the field through classroom presentations to the Child and Youth Care and Social Work students at Mount Royal University during this period.

Prior to this time, I coordinated the Recruit Training program and facilitated the Life Skills Delivery Techniques class to youth workers at the Alberta Solicitor General Staff Training Academy in Edmonton from 1999 to 2009. Towards the end of my tenure as the coordinator of the training program, I participated on the 10-member Youth Worker Recruit Training Review Committee. In 2007, I served on the Government of Alberta's Supervisor Certificate Review Team and continued in this role until 2009, lending valuable supervisory expertise to the 20-person group responsible for shaping a concrete learning foundation for new supervisors. Together, we established ways of measuring the learning curves of new supervisors during this developmental process and created a solid foundation for overall learning, mentoring, and feedback delivery.

In 2003, I was appointed to the Chair of the Youth Advisory Committee at CYOC and continued to serve in that capacity until I retired in 2015.   My role was to model a caring "voice" for troubled youth between the ages of 12 and 18 years. This role was and has been very dear to my heart. I have always and will always have time to teach and relate to young people through acts of kindness and service.

By 2011, I became a professional volunteer mentor at the Calgary Centre for Newcomers (CCN). Through my mentorship, I had an opportunity to aid, guide, educate, and connect professional newcomers in Calgary to resources that aided in securing employment in their fields, which reduced the stress of their settlement in this country. I was involved with the CCN for four years.

Awards and Recognition

For my contributions to my profession and professional communities, I have been recognized with the following awards, which I received with the humblest gratitude:

In 2008, I received the "Correctional Exemplary Services *Medal* Award" for long standing service both inside and outside of the workplace. In 2009, I received the "Solicitor General and Public Security Leadership Award".   In 2015, I was honoured again for my work in corrections with the "Correctional

Exemplary Service *Bar* Award" presented by the office of the Governor General of Canada. Also in 2015, I received the "Justice and Solicitor General Milestone Award" for 30 years of public service.

I have built my life around SERVICE. Furthermore, I have been amply rewarded for my service, not just through the

recognitions that I have received, but I've been truly blessed to see lives changed and the people around me and within my influence succeed in life. This is my most treasured award above all else.

. . . .

For centuries, people all over the planet have given of their time, talents, and resources. Extensive research has been conducted to explore the effects of volunteering on individuals who have chosen to give of themselves. Most recently, BC Living — a Health and Wellness publication — reported that studies have shown that working in the service of others enhances physical, mental, and emotional wellbeing. Aside from feeling good about helping others, people who routinely assist others often benefit from reduced risk of cardiovascular diseases, improved immune function, and expanded social connections. With an expanded social network, the Public Health Agency of Canada reports that people who remain actively engaged in life tend to have better, overall mental health. In addition, they are more capable of coping with life's transitions than those who don't. Volunteering has also been shown to decrease anxiety and depression, improve self-esteem, and diminish the effects of stress. Giving of oneself through time, talents, and resources has far-reaching benefits for the giver.

For young people, volunteering opens many doors for networking. Through these acts of service, youth access opportunities that enable them to learn and develop skills that they can then add to resumes as well as serve as an important reference for future employment. They also gain valuable work experience through the process, and expand their horizons by meeting new people. Their involvement may even lead to in-house training or scholarships. Finally, it boosts young people's self-esteem, as they feel needed. Volunteering as a young person provides valuable, long-term benefits for the future.

Ultimately, through volunteering and giving of yourself in SERVICE, you are making a difference in the world! I am a strong and fulfilled woman in a large part because of my focus on and dedication to positively influencing and uplifting the people around me and within my communities. I am truly blessed!

"Not all of us can do great things.
But we can do small things
with great love."[11]

---

[11] Often attributed to Mother Teresa. However, as written, they are not her authentic words.

Chapter 9

MARCHING ON

On May 20, 2015, I left my employer of over thirty years as a civil servant. It was a sudden departure, a premature goodbye. Yet in retrospect, it was a timely moment to begin the next leg of my life's journey. That closed door opened up the opportunity to write the next chapter of my life and free up the utmost amount of time to continue to live my life fully.

As the saying goes, when life hands you lemons, you make lemonade out of it! Although my employer rewrote the terms of my employment contract, and it was rescinded shortly thereafter when a new government took over the affairs of the province, I chose not to return. I accepted my early retirement as part of my destiny.

I have always believed that things happen for a reason. My early retirement was the push I needed to move on in my life – a push to embark on a new journey, a chance to do things that I had only dreamt of doing but never had enough time or the courage to do...yet. But now, I do – and I have risen to the challenge of embracing this new chapter of my life with courage, joy, and anticipation.

Enjoying Family

At the time of my early retirement, my oldest grandson, Ezra, was fifteen months old and my younger grandson, Caxton, was seven months old. I started my days on this new journey of mine planning how to spend more time with them. Spring was in the air, summer was fast approaching, and plans were made to spend quality time outdoors with my handsome grandbabies. These precious times were and continue to be cherished very much!

Ezra had just started going to daycare when I retired, so we hung out as often as time permitted. His cousin, Caxton, was not yet in daycare, so we spent countless moments together until he turned two and started daycare, attending the same one as Ezra. Those two love each other and enjoy each other's company immensely.

It has been fun watching Caxton mimic and learn from his "Glamma" as I am called. Watching him develop his languages (English and Yoruba) and witnessing his personality bloom like a rose has brought me such joy, making me realize just how blessed I am for the opportunity to be a part of these innocent, human beings' lives. I look forward to many more years of excitement, creating memories with all my wonderful grandbabies.

I have to say that my retirement has provided my husband some 'fringe benefits' as well, to which he reluctantly agrees. Being at home regularly has allowed us to spend more quality time together, focus more attention on each other's wellbeing, and cherish the joys of family life and festivities. My time is now my own – I decide – and it has enhanced my relationship with husband and the rest of my family.

Travel

As an adventurous person, I have always loved travelling. I want to see and know about as many places in the world as my time on earth permits me to. I left Nigeria short of my twentieth birthday and travelled to Canada. Within Canada, I have visited many cities and little towns within Alberta, travelled as far west as beautiful Victoria, British Columbia, with many vacation stops in that beautiful province. I have experienced the beauty and warm hospitality of this great nation of Canada through visits to Quebec City, Montreal,

Toronto, Ottawa, Winnipeg, Saskatoon, and Fort Smith in the Northwest Territories (NWT).

While many places I've visited in Canada are well known and recognized, Fort Smith is not. It is a small, government town of approximately 2500 people (2011 census) located on the NWT/Alberta border. In fact, it is the southernmost community in the NWT.

You must wonder why I traveled to a seemingly insignificant place such as Fort Smith. As usual, I was looking for more challenges and professional advancement. During my search, I stumbled upon a program management position for a minimum-security women's institution operated by the federal government. In my quest for advancement, I applied and was granted a telephone interview. They must have been impressed, for they extended an invitation for a personal interview to be conducted in Fort Smith, with the government paying for my flight and accommodation as a matter of course.

This little town was so unique and breathtaking. From its people, to its tiny airport, its distance from major cities, its weather, to its sunrise and sunset, this town was decidedly distinctive. I was in Fort Smith in early April, yet there was a ton of snow all the way up to my knees. But because the sun shone so brightly and intensely, the resulting snowmelt created water puddles everywhere. The residents didn't appear to mind one bit, as everybody wore winter boots up to their knees. People also drove trucks to help them navigate through the snow and puddles. In fact, I did not see a single car during my stay. Because supplies were brought in by water in the summer and flown in during the winter, everything was very costly. It was quite the town.

My interview in Fort Smith went very well, and I was subsequently offered the job. After taking stock of my family life in Calgary, especially what it would mean with regard to displacing my children and disrupting my husband's employment, I decided that the stakes were too high for the promotion and upgrade in pay. Nevertheless, I got to see Fort Smith, Northwest Territories! It was such a stunning area of Canada!

I hope to visit other places in Canada now that I have more time. One day soon, I plan to make my way to Nova Scotia and the Maritimes. Maybe it'll be a road trip with a group of friends. That would be awesome! I am more than ready to explore my chosen country some more in the years ahead.

I have enjoyed all the places I have been to. I have been to the United States many times throughout the years. My first trip was taken only six months after my arrival in Canada when I went to visit my brother in South Bend, Indiana. Since that first visit, I have traveled to many different places throughout the States: Chicago (many times) - Houston - Washington, DC - Maryland - New York - Hawaii - Orlando - San Diego -

Washington State - Idaho - Salt Lake City - Palm Springs and Las Vegas (both, many times). Rounding up the North American continent, I've visited a few parts of Mexico including Puerto Vallarta, Cancun, and Los Cabos. Internationally, I have visited: London, England - Rome, Italy - Amsterdam, Holland - Frankfurt, Germany - Dubai, United Arab Emirates - Panama City, Panama. The unique cultures, the people, the food, the languages, the architecture, and the museums all thrill me. Above all, the street scenes capture my attention the most. My husband and I both absolutely love the street scenes. We particularly love to check out the various markets and visit and mingle with the locals, for I love to ask questions. I have a need to know, which also explains why I love to travel so much.

I have so many memories of the places I have been to, but I must say that I particularly fell in love with Panama. Panama is a country in Central America that has coastlines on both the Caribbean Sea and the Pacific Ocean. It is located between the nations of Colombia and Costa-Rica. A people of diverse heritages populate Panama including Native Panamanians, Afro Panamanians, Mulattos, Whites, and Mestizos. Each people group have their own language(s), but Spanish is the official language. By the time we visited Panama in 2011, the English language was beginning to spread throughout the nation due to a flourishing tourism economy. While the ruins of General Manuel Noriega's brutal era and the invasion of Panama by the

United States in 1989 were still evident, there was optimism amongst the people everywhere. Foreign investments in ocean view, high-rise condominiums and city skyscrapers abound. We went on guided tours through the jungles and wetlands where we saw rare birds, various species of small animals, waterfalls, and natural hot springs. The local markets were filled with colourful arts and crafts, aromatic and flavourful foods, and an abundance of seafood. I never got tired of eating the seafood! The weather was very hot and humid; therefore, we went on our tours very early in the day, returning to our resort by mid-day. By then, we'd see children in a vast array of different school uniforms with their school bags, walking in groups here, there, and everywhere in the hot, blazing sun. I saw my younger self – growing up in Lagos, Nigeria – in those kids. I enjoyed the green, lush, tropical vegetation, which also reminded me of my childhood in high school at my boarding school where I dreaded the drenching, fatigue-effects of the high humidity along with the insects, especially the mosquitos, that came with it. I thoroughly enjoyed and have the fondest memories of Panama, and I would love to visit again.

Immediately after retirement, traveling was on my agenda. As mentioned, my husband and I enjoyed a couple of road trips in western Canada, one with friends and another by ourselves. We relished the freedom to explore the great country of Canada this way. Travel is definitely in our future.

ParenTeen Connections

In 2015, I launched ParenTeen Connections – a Life Skills, Workshop, Facilitation, Coaching program for teens and parents. In the first year, two classes consisting of junior high and high school students were held. The experiences were very invigorating for me! It has been especially satisfying to read the feedback from the youth.

<u>2015 – Grades 6-9 – Summer Camp Feedback (Excerpts)</u>

"I gained knowledge about values and decision making and would like to learn about personal safety in [a] future class."

"It helped me know how to make the right decision...I would like to gain confidence in interacting with others and dealing with peer pressure."

"I learnt how to act amongst people and how to choose my future job...I would like to learn different ways to study."

"I learned how to make proper decisions and values...I want the program to be a week long or more than two days...I would like to learn about career choices and universities; dating and peer

pressure; the right way to save money...bring in speakers like doctors, lawyers, stylists, designers, veterinarians, and others."

"I gained knowledge about where values come from and that one's values determine what is right from wrong...I'd like to learn more about self-esteem, dealing with stress, personal/health care, and stopping arguments."

"Learnt how to make smart decisions, keep [my] own values, and made new friends...I'll (sic) like to have topics on anti-bullying, internet safety/dating, and sexuality and peer pressure".

"I learned about different values and [it] helped me to make decisions...I want the program to be three days. I want to learn more about the Canadian Charter of Rights and Freedoms, how to stop peer pressure and gain self esteem "

"I'll (sic) like to learn more about drug abuse and peer pressure, and I will recommend this program to my friends because it helps to build good character."

"I would recommend this program because it should help with social skills and personal development."

"I learnt how much my decisions are influenced by my values and people around me...I would like to learn more about youth and the law, career choices, and conflict resolution...I will recommend this class because we learn and have fun, too."

"I want to learn more about freedom and how to deal with school issues."

"I learn (sic) about making good choices, and I will recommend this program because it teaches some things that can help us now [and] in the future."

Fall 2015 – Grades 9-12 – Dating Workshop Feedback (Excerpts)

"I learned about many types of relationships, the meaning of consent, and how to protect myself."

"I gained knowledge about healthy vs. unhealthy relationships and how to protect myself from sexually transmitted diseases."

"I learnt about domestic abuse and positive relationships."

"[I learned] How important consent is in a relationship before sex and how easy it is to get an STI. I will recommend this

program to my friends because they get to talk about those things they may not [be] 100% comfortable talking about."

"I learned about safety, choices, dating, and sexual consent."

"I learnt how to know if someone is being abused, sexuality, and ways to live a healthy life."

"I learned about what to look for when thinking about dating. I learned about safe sex and how to choose abstinence. I would recommend the program to my friends because you get together and learn things that will help us in the future."

"I gained the ability to identify an unhealthy relationship and [the] qualities to look for in my future partner. The class was amazing and entertaining. The presenter is awesome and informed."

"I gained understanding of consent, sexuality, and condoms. I will (sic) like to learn more about university, future aspirations, and how to define success. Engineering, medicine, and law are not the only way."

"I gained awareness about all types of abuse and how to practice safer sex. The program was very educational and

255

informative – information that can be applied to everyday life. I can apply this in the future and [in the] present."

"I learned that consent is necessary and why some people stay in abusive relationships. The program was very interactive and fun. I want to talk more about dating."

"I learned what to look for in a date and would like to know how to keep a relationship."

Other Community Work

My commitment to inspire and empower young immigrants, their parents, and others factors prominently into my future. As such, my voluntary services in 2016, among others, included group work facilitation for the Calgary Catholic Immigrant Services (CCIS) and the Calgary Bethany Chapel's Community and Women's Ministries.

*July 22, 2016 – "Moji Taiwo presented a workshop "**Rising Above**" to the youth of the CCIS Immigrant Youth Outreach Project. The presentation provided a platform for the youth to openly discuss the barriers faced by immigrants and create positive solutions to overcome these issues. Moji was great with the youth. Her ideas* *were concise and easy for the youth to understand, and she kept them engaged by drawing from her own experiences as both an immigrant and a Youth Worker. The feedback we received from some of the youth was that they felt connected, inspired and the presentation motivated them to work hard to be successful in Canada. Thank you."*

Amanda – Youth Counselor Immigrant Youth Outreach Project – CCIS

*January 2016 – **Time-out and Touch-base Parenting Group** – "Thanks so much, Moji; I really enjoyed the session – I know the ladies did as well! Such a pleasure to meet you. I look forward to our next session as well. Take care."*

Mary – Community & Women's Ministries Director, Bethany Chapel

Here are some excerpts from reviews from the 2017 Summer Camp Coaching Sessions:

"The knowledge that stood out front and centre for me during the mentorship classes and throughout the summer – that is the importance of basic character in yourself and in the people that you choose to have relationships with."

"From our weekly sessions, I have learnt the following:

1) That I'm going to start [a] TFSA and a trading account hopefully by next week.

2) All the career options I wish I knew before going into university. I'll teach all my loved ones that they have options before they go into university.

3) How to communicate, especially with the little drama (role-play) we did. I used that on a kid yesterday, and it worked like a charm.

"Thank you so much for the lessons!!!"

"The classes we had as a group has (sic) benefited me because I had no idea about them before. Money management was a huge part because I didn't know about the interest rate and the way a credit card works properly. Also, what is needed and important about relationships. Thank you for infusing words of wisdom in us for our future."

"Before I say one thing I've learned, I would like to thank you for the time you took to teach us the things you did. I greatly appreciate it. The one thing I learned and found most value in was the information on credit cards. Before the session, I didn't know exactly how they worked, but after I understood...you can get a credit card, but you should be able to pay the money before the interest rate period hits so you do not get into debt. I *also appreciated all the life lessons, laughs, and the discussions you shared with us. Thank you."*

"One thing that I've learned in this (sic) sessions that we had this summer is the importance of saving money and investing. The cool thing about investing is that you can put an amount of money in the bank and get money on top of that just for putting it in the bank. I also learned that it's important that, before I spend money, I should take 10% out to save and work my spending in the 90% of my earnings."

"I learned better ways to communicate effectively, and I learned more about money management. Thank you for your time and have a great day!"

"I've learned to not limit myself to one career path. Now there are so many things I can become that can combine all of my skills and interests. So I should not just chase a job that provides a lot of money, but instead follow my passion."

"What I've gained during these classes are the knowledge of how to spend my money and use it more wisely, and how to take my money [that] I have now and grow it into more money for the future."

Modeling

Since retirement, I have also ramped up my modeling engagements. Now that I'm more available, I've had more time

for photo shoots, including shoots for print and video commercials and stock photos. I'm on a bus shelter and in print and videos somewhere in the world. I also got to appear as an Extra on Fargo, the television series, and Damnation, an American television series (2017) shot in and around Calgary. Life is good!

Credit: Hero Images

. . . .

My adopted home of Canada is a country that does not claim to have a perfect system, but it strives to create a (near) perfect system. It is a country with functioning infrastructures geared towards the comfort of all her citizens. It is a country rich in history, starting with her First Nations people and the cultures of her earliest settlers, all the way to its native-born citizens and its most recent immigrants. Canada is a country where I can be whomever I want to be...and I have done so to the fullest with all that I have in me.

Having the time, courage, and the tenacity to work on this book has been a journey on its own. I wouldn't have been able to embark on this project fully had I been working full-time. I still occupy my time and self productively, and I enjoy doing all the things I do on a daily basis, including the fun stuff. Yes, I am retired from my formal career, but I am not retired from life!

For my future, I plan to continue to expand my horizons through exploration in all aspects of my life, be it family, community, or travel. And I will always follow my passion for enriching lives, for investing in community service, and for living live fully.

I'm not tired, nor will I ever be, of being a purposeful contributing member of society. I'm certainly not tired of touching people's lives in a positive way. I am all about leaving an everlasting impression Smiles, Joy, Happiness, Kindness, and Love – in my path.

Quite simply...I am incredibly BLESSED!

First Christmas Picture with Grandchildren

2014

Thank You to My Sponsors!

I would like to give special thanks to those Sponsors – you know who you are – who have partnered with me to publish this book. Your trust and belief in my story having value and impact is greatly appreciated. May you be richly blessed in return!

Moji Taiwo

"Living in Calgary for over 40 years, I know this city like the back of my hands. All immigrants can have a peace of mind knowing that someone like myself can help them find a suitable housing for their family before they even land here. My dream for all immigrants coming is for them to own a piece of this great land. As a Top Producing Real Estate Agent, no matter where someone is coming from or if they want to first rent, buy, sell or even relocate, I can help them find the perfect property. Like Ms. Taiwo has said in her book, it's all about leaving an everlasting impression, and if that means helping my fellow immigrants to achieve one piece of their Canadian dream, I would be honoured to help them with that dream of property ownership."

I am successful because I produce RESULTS!

Ms. Tokunbo Davidson

Top Producing Realtor

Century 21 Bravo Realty

homes@toknborealty.com

Cell: + 1 (403) 437-4379

Office: +1 (403) 796-7653